5/17/23
$5.w

The Sanity of Satire

The Sanity of Satire

Surviving Politics One Joke at a Time

AL GINI AND ABRAHAM SINGER

ROWMAN & LITTLEFIELD
Lanham • Boulder • New York • London

Published by Rowman & Littlefield
An imprint of The Rowman & Littlefield Publishing Group, Inc.
4501 Forbes Boulevard, Suite 200, Lanham, Maryland 20706
www.rowman.com

6 Tinworth Street, London SE11 5AL, United Kingdom

Library of Congress Cataloging-in-Publication Data

Names: Gini, Al, 1944– author. | Singer, Abraham A., author.
Title: The sanity of satire : surviving politics one joke at a time / Al Gini and
    Abraham Singer.
Description: Lanham : Rowman & Littlefield, [2020] | Includes bibliographical
    references and index. | Summary: "Political humor and satire are, perhaps, as
    old as comedy itself, and they are crucial to our society and collective sense
    of self. In a poignant, pithy, but not ponderous manner, Al Gini and Abraham
    Singer delve into satire's history to rejoice in its triumphs and watch its
    development from ancient graffiti to the latest late-night talk show"— Provided
    by publisher.
Identifiers: LCCN 2020011925 (print) | LCCN 2020011926 (ebook) | ISBN
    9781538129715 (cloth) | ISBN 9781538129722 (epub)
Subjects: LCSH: Political satire, American—History and criticism. | American
    wit and humor—History and criticism. | Wit and humor—Psychological
    aspects. | United States—Politics and government—Humor.
Classification: LCC PS430 .G48 2020 (print) | LCC PS430 (ebook) | DDC
    817/.609—dc23
LC record available at https://lccn.loc.gov/2020011925
LC ebook record available at https://lccn.loc.gov/2020011926

Two professors walk into a bar . . .

To Sherry and Luisa:
They make us laugh, and we love them for that!

Satire is a tool. It's a way of reaching out and putting your arm around something, pointing at something, and saying, "Isn't that funny, strange, and awkward that we do that? Maybe we should think about this a little more and perhaps do something about it?"

—CASSAR, SOUTH AFRICAN COMIC

CONTENTS

DISCLAIMER

The reader will notice there is no mention of the COVID-19 pandemic or the world's responses to it in the pages that follow. That is because this book was written and submitted for publication prior to the coronavirus outbreak. Way back then—in the "before-time," as a friend likes to call it—people used to socialize in groups and laugh together, sometimes even slapping each other on the back or high-fiving, in various ways that would violate the social distance protocols with which we are now all too familiar. Back then, if someone said something "went viral," they were probably talking about a funny video on YouTube, not an actual virus.

In this book, we try to show how deeply connected comedy and satire are with the human condition. This claim has not been altered by COVID-19. On the contrary, the coronavirus experience has only emphasized further how important comedy and satire are for our lives even (and especially) in the face of world-historic tragedy.

PROLOGUE

"Up until now, comedy didn't usually write itself. It was a hard job! Not anymore, thanks to you know who!"

—LEWIS BLACK

Let's start out with some basics. One, humor—from pie-in-the-face slapstick to sophisticated cerebral satire—seems to be a universal feature of the human condition. Two, there is no Platonic ideal of the perfect joke or the perfect joke formula. Three, different folks like different jokes. Four, when you have to diagram a joke, show how it works, and explain why it's funny, then the joke ceases to be funny. Five, comedy is a rough game. Risking offense is part of that game.

Six, satire is a species of joke telling. Satire intentionally uses humor to draw attention to actions, issues, and ideas that need modification or correction. More than just telling jokes for the purpose of pleasure, delight, or momentary escapism, satire entertains in order to critique current unacceptable personal or social conditions or situations. According to Scottish philosopher Francis Hutcheson, satire uses humor, rather than mere haranguing, to achieve civilized ends: "Men have been laughed out of faults which a sermon could not reform."[1]

Different from comedians as entertainers, satirists choose to be contrarians, confrontational, and critics of the status quo. The cliché that "comedians are like canaries in a coal mine" should really read "satirists are the true canaries in a coal mine." The job of the canary is to warn the miners of the otherwise undetectable buildup of toxic gases (methane or carbon monoxide) in the mine by suddenly dying! While, metaphorically speaking, satirists occasionally die onstage, their intended job is to evoke a warning and possibly provoke change. According to comedian Margaret Cho, what satirists do is take a topic that's dark and difficult and, by turning it into a joke, make it more legible and make the audience more amenable to critically reflecting upon it.[2]

Although satire can take any particular aspect of the human condition as its subject, historically its primary focus has been on *zoon politikon* (humankind as a political animal). For example, in *The Clouds* (circa 423 BCE), the Athenian playwright Aristophanes comically eviscerated—by means of sexual innuendo, plenty of fart jokes, and more than a few oversized phalluses—Socrates's growing influence and popularity in the political and social life of Athenian democracy. Our individual and collective preoccupation with all things political seems to be a constant feature of the human condition. The near-universal impulse to satirize our political worlds, which seems to transcend time and place, is a consequence of this fact.

In current-day America, this general impulse trains itself on one target. Unless you have been living in a hermetically sealed biosphere without any access to the outside world, then you are aware that since 2014, the collective attention of this nation has been focused on one particular person: the president of the United States of America, Donald J. Trump.

Political pundits of every persuasion are in lockstep on at least one issue: Whether you are a supporter or a detractor (no one is neutral!), as a nation we are riveted to the spectacle of the Trump presidency. Many of those who support him believe that he will do what he promised to do: "Make America Great Again!" His detractors fear that "the norms of our republic are eroding quicker than Miami beachfront property!"[3]

But whether you like him or loathe him—the man, the brand, the candidate, the president has proven to be a delicious and desirable target of commentary and critique. And professional satirists are working overtime to keep up with the wealth of material daily available to them.

Stay calm, dear reader, although it will be difficult to do so: this text is not an exercise in "Trump bashing." Rather, it's an attempt to fully understand the nature and use of humor and satire in our personal, professional, and public lives. We want to examine the ways that humor and satire help us deal with "the good, the bad, and the ugly" aspects of our collective existence. Our goal is to both edify and entertain. You can't really understand the political importance of humor unless you also *get* the jokes! Deep philosophical musing and laughter are both recommended and encouraged.

Neither of us is trained in linguistics, the philosophy of humor, or the history of comedic literature and criticism. Gini is trained as a moral philosopher; Singer as a political theorist. We both work at a business school where we teach business ethics and leadership. While these areas of scholarship are not unrelated to satire and comedy—as we'll see, comedy has important moral aspects and serves important political functions— this book did not grow out of our academic expertise. Instead, it grew from the simple fact that every time the two of us got together, ostensibly to talk about a lecture or a new article in *Business Ethics Quarterly*, the conversation would quickly turn to comedy and jokes: "Did you see Chris Tucker's new special?" "What's that great Groucho line about dancing with the cows?" And, of course, "Did ya hear the one about . . . ?" Indeed, even when we were talking about writing this prologue, this one came up:

A cannibal was walking through his town and came upon a restaurant opened by a fellow cannibal. Feeling somewhat hungry, he sat down and looked over the menu: Broiled English Professor $10—Fried Lawyer $15—Baked Politician $100. The cannibal called the waiter over and asked, "Why such a price difference for the politician?" The waiter replied, "Have you ever tried to clean one?"

We both wanted to write this book because we both love jokes and the craft of comedy. As our students can also attest, we both think we're pretty funny (whether others do is another story entirely, as both our wives can attest). But we also both think that comedy is important for reasons beyond mere entertainment. Personally, comedy has helped us through dark times, and socially we believe that comedy has the power to bind people together and help them overcome the obstacles inherent to politics and collective action. Satirizing the world we inhabit—with its cast of asshole politicians, nosy neighbors, prejudiced citizens, and the like—is a crucial part of how we manage to live and thrive as thinking, caring, connected people.

Satire has been something of a lifeline for many people today, a way to deal with the crazed state of politics that we face. This is good and important, but it's not the only important aspect of satirical humor. The book aims not just to think about satire in terms of Trump but to celebrate it as a comedic, personal, and social achievement. We talk about Trump, sure (see chapter 1), but we also talk about other things: how satire is important for our individual sanity (chapter 2), its role in improving citizenship and democracy (chapter 3), and the way women and Jews (chapters 4 and 5) have used satire to speak to particular experiences. We also want to put our philosopher caps on a bit and ask some moral questions: Are there things that are off limits for comedy (chapter 6)? Do we perhaps make too many jokes as a society (chapter 7)? But our aim is to always do so with reference to and examples of actual jokes and the jokers who cracked them.

Humor, satire, laughter—this book is about how we use such things as tools to both cope with and improve upon our far-from-ideal world. Jokes aren't always enough, of course, but they can help. In the words of sage, guru, and (as PBS documentarian Robert Trachtenburg called him) "political analyst extraordinaire" Mel Brooks, "Sometimes the only response to the absurdity of life and politics is to laugh at it."[4]

CHAPTER 1

Trumping Trump

"When I was a boy, I was told anyone could become president; and [now] I'm beginning to believe it."
—CLARENCE DARROW

According to longtime *SNL* comedy writer Jack Handey, jokes are, by their very nature, both perishable and parochial.[1] That is, jokes—no matter how well crafted and funny—are not funny forever. Jokes are produced for, and specifically play to, a particular audience and context. All jokes have a very short "shelf life" because all jokes depend on familiarity with items, issues, and personalities in the news and a general grasp of the zeitgeist of which they are a part. Jokes need to be fresh and somehow stand out in order to have cultural impact/currency.

Today, no one tells sizzling sarcastic quips about Rock Hudson being the male romantic lead in a series of Doris Day films (from 1959 to 1964) even though it was well known, at least in Hollywood circles, that he was gay. And we know for a fact that there's not one working comic today who can bring an audience to a fever pitch of laughter with a number of graphic, salacious stories about the adulterous behavior of Elizabeth Taylor and Richard Burton while they were filming the 1963 blockbuster *Cleopatra*.

Jokes always have a real-world referent. Jokes arise, emerge, and evolve out of lived experiences. Life itself is the cause and/or the catalyst for comedy. For example, Ricky Gervais tells a little joke about the recent political controversy surrounding the taking down of confederate military statues in the North and the South. In order to avoid public rancor or the possibility of violence, Gervais suggests, instead of taking them down, new plaques should be affixed to the statues: "A great general, but a bit of a racist!"[2] Clearly, the sociopolitical humor of this joke only makes sense after the summer of 2016 and the protests and riots that occurred in a number of cities and college campuses regarding the political correctness of honoring individuals and a cause that supported slavery in America.

The particulars of life establish the parameters of comedy. Jokes are dependent on time, place, the circumstance of the joker, and the taste and temperament of the audience. Comedy is both an intellectual and an emotional event, and both the "teller" and the "told" have to be on the same cultural page. Otherwise, joke telling is a purely theoretical exercise. And, of course, because lifestyles, languages, and cultures are so diverse and ever changing, there is no such thing as a pure joke, a universal joke, or a joke that would make sense and be funny to everyone.

Part-time stand-up comic and full-time philosopher Ted Cohen argues that all jokes are conditional—that is, all jokes have conditional requirements connecting the teller and the audience, or common knowledge, common background, common language, and common cultural presuppositions, prejudices, and myths. When a joke works, it's because the joker is telling a story and using assumptions, knowledge, cultural references, and a background that an audience understands and knows how to react and respond to. The most elemental reason why jokes do not work is because we do not all share the same life experiences, the same frames of reference. In the end, we are a society divided by different tastes because we are a society of different backgrounds and experiences.[3] The conditional nature of joke telling explains why comedy is so subjective and why the popularity of jokes and comics tends to be community specific, generational, or niche based.

Joke telling is like popular music in this regard. Popular or commercial music primarily speaks to a very specific audience, a very specific demographic slice of the total pie. That is why most parents and children are surprised and amazed by what each of them considers listenable, enjoyable, danceable popular songs and singers. In the mid-1950s, for example, parents were saying to their kids, "Elvis screams, Sinatra sings!" Many of today's parents feel the same way about the difference between Elton John and someone like Nas or Post Malone.

While particular jokes are triggered and connected to a specific person or persons and a particular time and place, categories of jokes—types of jokes that share the same or similar general topics—have a much longer and deeper lifespan and are transcultural in nature, no matter how disquieting, plebian, or personal they might be. Jokes about disgusting or divine bodily functions, jokes about drinking, drugs, God, marriage, kids, money, poverty, success, wealth, work, food, friends, politics, power, and so forth: while any specific joke about any of these things requires a specific audience, all of these themes and topics, and many more, have a certain universal cachet.

According to Gershon Legman, underground sexual theoretician and indefatigable encyclopedia of dirty jokes, the most popular form of joke is sex jokes. In his magnum opus, *Rationale of the Dirty Joke*, Legman claims that all cultures in all centuries have had an oral and/or written tradition of sexual humor and joke telling. Legman asserts that sexual jokes are part of human culture because sexuality, in all of its varied and peculiar manifestations, is an elemental part of human nature itself.[4]

However, because we are, by nature, codependent and communal animals, sex jokes are not the only universal sort of joke. Political jokes seem to be just as prevalent throughout human history. Soon after our ribald reveries concerning copulation, fellatio, and cunnilingus, more often than not we turn to kvetching about, defaming, or simply commenting on power, politics, and (perhaps especially) the personalities of particular politicians. In America, for example, we have made a minor art form out of holding up the commander in chief to merciless analysis or critique. History tells us that there were plenty of comments about George Washington's expensive taste in carriages and his bad teeth. There was a lot of talk about Thomas Jefferson being a womanizer and an adulterer. People told jokes about John Quincy Adams's outrageous habit of swimming nude in the Potomac River. People regularly commented on Abraham Lincoln's ungainly height and openly called him a "long-armed ape." We made fun of William Howard Taft's being too fat for his bathtub and "Silent Calvin" Coolidge's being too quiet. We smirked at Ronald Reagan's forgetfulness and perfect pompadour. And we were both shocked and titillated by JFK's and Bill Clinton's amorous predilections.

But never before have the particular and the categorical elements of comedy come together with such ferocity, velocity, and volume as has occurred since the candidacy and subsequent election of Donald J. Trump as the forty-fifth president of the United States. Trump has transformed the day-to-day conduct of the office of the presidency, rewritten the rules of engagement with foreign nations as well as Congress, and completely altered presidential communications and the president's relationship to the American public. In rewriting the rules of politics and resetting the rules of presidential demeanor and decorum, Trump is directly responsible for engendering a tsunami of political jokes and satirical bits. Comedians are no longer just taking occasional potshots at presidential politics and Mr. Trump's public demeanor. Rather, the president's words and behavior have become the entire focus of their individual performances and are often literally the main storyline of most late-night TV talk shows. To many, this is like a comedy gold rush. As *The Daily Show*'s Roy Wood Jr. put it, "An administration that's not as wacky, it's a bone carcass in the middle of the desert that everybody's trying to pick a little punch line off of. The Trump administration is a fucking beached whale that everybody can eat from."[5]

For others, the Trump presidency is comedy hell. Longtime comedian and political satirist Lewis Black has complained that the "Age of Trump" has taken the fun out of being a comic. After all, said Black, "how can you write or come up with lines, gags, and fuck-ups funnier than the shit that comes out of Washington and the White House every day? How can you write jokes that are funnier than the facts? You don't have to make stuff up anymore. Just read the headlines and repeat the quote." Black goes on to lament, "Where's the personal pride and dignity in that? I'm getting out of this business. It's not fun to be a comic anymore."[6] And yet, perhaps, to paraphrase a line from Shakespeare, "Methinks the gentlemen protests too much!" Or is Black just being meta-satirical about the surfeit of material now available to him and those like him who practice the art of satire?

But Black does raise a serious issue: "How do you satirize the satirical?"[7] Obviously, this has not proven to be a problem for a lot of other working comics.

Putting aside partisan politics and personal predilections for a moment, we think that it's fair to say that many were surprised by Mr. Trump's success in the Republican primaries and shocked by his election to the presidency. (According to some very serious and not-at-all funny political observers, Trump was too.) Love him or hate him, Trump's demeanor, his brashness and braggadocio, his iconoclastic pronouncements, his writ-large unorthodox behavior, and his over-the-top style and manner make him a natural target for media scrutiny and catalyst for controversy. The fact is, Trump the man, Trump the brand, Trump the president is a natural lightning rod for commentary and criticism and offers satirists a broad palette of comic possibilities. He is, simply put, a perfect comedic target!

It is interesting to note that Jon Stewart announced his retirement from *The Daily Show* some time before Trump officially announced his intention to enter the Republican primaries. One night before his final show (August 6, 2015), Stewart looked into the camera with a sad face and queried something to the effect of "What was I thinking, with Trump running? This will be the easiest job in the world."

While Stewart was only feigning personal disappointment and regret, in fact Trump has proven to be both a catalyst and a boon for political comedy and satire. So far, Trump has inspired two half-hour sitcoms: Comedy Central's live-action *The President Show* and Showtime's animated *Our Cartoon President*. And as we will turn to shortly, Trump's presidency has coincided with a radical increase in the ratings and viewership of comedy TV flagship *Saturday Night Live*, as well as the opening monologues and the general content of all the major late-night TV programming.

But, even before candidate Trump entered our collective consciousness, there was a show on HBO that fictionally anticipated, foreshadowed, and, in fact, predicted the fallacies, falsities, faux pas, and foolishness of the Trump administration: HBO's must-see *VEEP* (2012–2019), starring six-time Emmy Award–winning actress Julia Louis-Dreyfus. On *VEEP*, Louis-Dreyfus inhabits the role of Selina Meyer, an overly indulged, narcissistic child of wealth and privilege who, after serving in Congress as a U.S. senator representing Maryland, decides to seek the nomination of her party for the presidency (motivated mostly by personal vanity). Once it becomes clear that achieving the nomination is impossible, she is offered, and accepts, the VP spot on the ticket. But to her chagrin, she quickly learns what Daniel Webster meant when he turned down the VP position: "I do not propose to be buried until I am dead." Undeterred, the show follows Meyer using her time in political limbo to plot, plan, and use every opportunity to achieve the position she neither deserves nor is qualified for: president of the United States.

Selina Meyer is without scruples, character, or any kind of moral compass. True North for her is a simple and repeated equation: me, myself, and I. Her personal sense of identity seems to be almost exclusively derived from public recognition and adulation. She seeks public fame and adulation by whatever means necessary, whether it be mendacity, duplicity, blackmail, attack ads, illicit fund-raising, promiscuity, intimidation, or even conspiring with a foreign government. (Imagine that!) From a historical perspective, the character of Selina Meyer is a combination of Niccolò Machiavelli ("I seek power for power's sake alone"), Joseph Goebbels ("If you tell the big lie often enough, it becomes the big truth"), and Mae West ("Is that a gun you have in your pocket, or are you just glad to see me?").

Somewhere about halfway through the series, the writers, producers, and cast began to worry or became concerned about the "over-the-top" burlesque nature of the show. They felt that they were pushing the boundaries of fiction too far. They feared that Selina's megalomania, flamboyant vulgarity, ruthlessness, and careless behavior would make her too extreme, too unbelievable, and too unlikable.[8]

And then along came Donald Trump, the candidate and the president, and the cast of *VEEP* were faced with a serious, if absurdly funny, question. How do you do political satire when the world of politics and the behavior of the president are crazier and funnier than anything you could have imagined? "Our show started out as political satire. . . . But now," said Louis-Dreyfus, "it feels more like a sobering documentary. . . . It's getting too hard to differentiate satire from reality."[9]

Think about it! *VEEP* is the story of an "opportunistic, short-tempered vulgarian who, by sheer determination and blind luck, rose to become the President of the United States."[10] Sound vaguely familiar? As comedian and cultural commentator Hasan Minhaj pointed out at the 2017 White House Correspondents' Dinner, "The news coming out of the White House is so stressful, I've been watching *House of Cards* just to relax."

Donald Trump (as of summer 2019) has tweeted more than forty-three thousand times.[11] He has used these tweets to establish or change foreign policy, to comment on the Kentucky Derby, to chastise Democratic members of Congress, to belittle CNBC, CNN, etc., etc., for posting "fake news," to point out that CNN's Chris Cuomo looks like a "chained lunatic" on TV and that African American reporter Don Lemon is "perhaps the dumbest person in broadcasting," to criticize NFL players for kneeling during the national anthem, to disinvite sports teams to the White House to celebrate their victory, to assert multiple times that more people attended his inauguration than attended President Barack Obama's, to accuse congressional opponent Elijah Cummings of Baltimore of representing a "disgusting rat and rodent infected mess,"[12] and, maybe most egregiously, to insinuate that four freshman congresswomen of color (Alexandria Ocasio-Cortez of New York, Ilhan Omar of Minnesota, Ayanna Pressley of Massachusetts, and Rashida Tlaib of Michigan) were not American, saying that if they didn't "like it here," they should "go back" to where they come from.[13]

During the Nixon administration (1969–1974) Pulitzer Prize–winning novelist Philip Roth blurted out in frustration and despair, "American craziness is so crazy that it is become impossible to write fiction anymore!"[14] Richard Nixon clearly caused havoc in America's body politic, but Nixon's level of craziness pales in comparison to the craziness engendered by the Trump presidency. It presents something of a paradox. You can't ignore him, but he's also hard to mock. He irresistibly invites satirists to take their best shot, while being so over-the-top that it's actually difficult to pull off well.

Although *VEEP* can be seen as the original flagship of the media flotilla engaged in the satirical assault against USS *Trump*, the main focus of attack is carried out by a squadron of nimble and fast-moving comedic destroyers and a few heavyweight cruisers in the form of daily and weekly TV shows. Since Trump entered the primary races, these shows have brought their satirical broadsides to bear on him. And since his election they have campaigned against him with zeal and devotion. They all seem to be motivated and energized by the belief that because of Trump the "norms of our republic are being eroded quicker than Miami beachfront property."[15]

Of course, political humor has long been part of the television landscape. For example, *Saturday Night Live (SNL)* has always satirically feasted on the foibles of politicians, politics, and, especially, presidential faux pas and policies. Over the years, one of its signature routines is having a specific cast member impersonate and parody the president in a season-long series of comedic situations. The string of famous "presidential" actors is notable: Chevy Chase played Gerald R. Ford, Dan Ackroyd played Jimmy Carter, Phil Hartman played Ronald Reagan, Dana Carvey played George H. W. Bush, Darrell

Hammond played Bill Clinton, Will Ferrell played George W. Bush, Jay Pharoah and Fred Armisen played Barack Obama, and, most recently, Alec Baldwin has delivered an over-the-top portrayal of Donald Trump. Baldwin has suggested that impersonating Trump is the easiest acting job he has ever had. Why? Because "Trump is the lead writer of *SNL*," said Baldwin. "Trump himself is responsible for nearly all of the content. . . . So [if Trump is displeased, and he was], I think Trump . . . has only himself to blame for that."[16]

Though Baldwin's Trump fits in a long lineage of impersonations, it also sticks out as particularly sharp toothed. Though *SNL* has always made fun of sitting presidents and politicians, the object of the satire has almost always been perceived character traits, mannerisms, and foibles—Ford the moron, Clinton the horndog, W. Bush the simpleton. Despite having political figures as characters in its sketches, *SNL*'s satire has not always been terribly *political*. Satirizing the policies, personnel decisions, and professional activities of the sitting president—that is, making fun of the president for what he is doing *as president*—though never absent, is relatively new as a preoccupation for *SNL*. This isn't just the case with sketches involving the president. "Weekend Update," now largely focused on satirizing real political events, used to be far more absurdist in content, dominated more by lines like "Generalissimo Francisco

Franco is still dead," "Jane, you ignorant slut," and "You guessed it: Frank Stallone" than by penetrating, sharp-knifed political critique.

SNL's evolution is not unique in this regard. Historically, late-night TV shows, going back to Steve Allen, Jack Paar, Johnny Carson, Jay Leno, Conan O'Brien, and David Letterman, have all taken their potshots at politics and politicians. But they were, for the most part, "one-off" jokes, part of the opening monologue and not the backbone or theme of that evening's show. And when they told a softball joke about a Democrat, more often than not it was quickly followed up with a similar type of joke about a Republican. Being "bipartisan" was a comedic necessity to maintain nightly viewership ratings.

Today's new crop of late-night hosts are intentionally and unavoidably much more political than their comedic predecessors. But the spectrum and depth of their political satire varies from host to host.

Jimmy Fallon (NBC) and, to a lesser extent, Jimmy Kimmel (ABC) have taken a more conservative approach to their regular, if not nightly, comedic reflections on Trump's personal demeanor and politics as president. Their respective nightly monologues are similar in tone and intent. They don't try to stroke political outrage or activism. They are not after political wisdom or reform. They seem to be following the model of both Johnny

Carson and Jay Leno: take a shot, go for the gag line, but don't beat them to death.

Stephen Colbert's (CBS) and Seth Meyers's (NBC) shows, however, have taken on the mantle of the legendary Knights Templar in their all-out holy crusade against the usurper of the presidency and the sacred American way of life. OK, so that's a little bit over the top. But both of these hosts use their shows in a direct, unrelenting, and unapologetic assault against all things Trump. Seth Meyers (former "Weekend Update" anchor and *SNL* head writer) is the calmer of the two, but his commentary is just as cutting as his fellow warrior's. For those late-late-night TV watchers, Meyer calmly and carefully—more in the manner of a mathematician than an activist—disassembles and deconstructs the logic (or lack thereof) in Trump's statements and policies.

On election night in 2016, Stephen Colbert wondered out loud whether political comedy was possible anymore. Well, it did survive, and Stephen Colbert has had something to do with that. Every night, playing the hybrid role of comedic master of ceremonies, political theorist, investigative reporter, and op-ed firebrand, Colbert attacks and dissects all things Trump. Sometimes the assault is only part of the opening monologue, and other times it lasts the length of the show. Colbert doesn't try to hide his personal beliefs and feelings, he doesn't deny his deep Catholic Democratic roots, and he makes it clear that although he's making jokes about Trump's politics and personal behavior, he's not kidding! Colbert has proven that not only is "Trump good for comedy," he's also great for Colbert's ratings. Colbert initially had difficulty in taking over Letterman's helm, suffering low viewership and harsh criticism (much of it self-generated). By November 2018, however, Nielsen's late-night ratings reported CBS's Colbert's viewership at 4.02 million, passing NBC's Jimmy Fallon at 2.76 million and ABC's Jimmy Kimmel at 2.35 million.[17]

Some of this change is surely due to the nature of American politics, which has become more polarizing and more central to many citizens' private identities. Bet-hedging humor with low political stakes is simply not as appealing to many today. There is much more of an appetite for edgier, opinionated, and strident satire that is unafraid to state a view—even a controversial one. However, this change is not entirely due to shifts in the audience's relationship to politics. It is also, importantly, due to how comedians see their role in political life.

We believe it is safe to argue that in today's America, the nature, tone, impact, and import of political comedy and satire have been forever altered by Jon Stewart, whose influence is most palpable and widespread. However, in addition to Stewart, Bill Maher deserves a lot of credit for altering the relationship between comedy, comedians, and politics. Both of these men have forever changed the rules of the comedy game through their trailblazing TV shows, as well as a cadre of successful apprentices and journeymen and -women who were groomed and developed on these shows. After them, "safe" political humor looks, well, safe, in the pejorative sense of the term.

In 1993, a new and struggling cable channel, Comedy Central, made Bill Maher the host and chief commentator of a show called *Politically Incorrect.* The show was a hit, and after three years it was picked up by ABC. Because of a controversy over some of Maher's comments regarding the 9/11 terrorist attacks—"We have been the cowards, lobbing cruise missiles from 2,000 miles away. That's cowardly. Staying in the airplane when it hits the building? Say what you want about it . . . not cowardly"[18]—the show was cancelled. In 2003, HBO relaunched Maher's TV career with the production of *Real Time with Bill Maher.* On this one-hour weekly show, which is still going strong, Maher attacks the news with pugilistic ferocity. He dices, disassembles, and tries to both illuminate and disable what he takes to be foibles and foolishness on the political/social/cultural scene. Although Maher is making fun of the contemporary political scene, he comes off as genuinely angry, "pissed off," and personally offended by it all.

Throughout the show, Maher's comments are without license or limits. He is more than willing—in fact, he seems eager—to figuratively decapitate any policies or politicians that invoke his ire. Moreover, he is completely open about this private life, predilections, and politics. He admits to being a progressive, an atheist, a drinker, a pothead, and a major financial patron of the Democratic Party, while also criticizing fellow travelers for what he perceives as hypocrisy, stupidity, or oversensitivity. Despite his progressive bona fides, Maher is also persona non grata in many progressive circles for unapologetic criticisms of religious people generally and organized Islam in particular, which many consider Islamophobia.

Maher makes no attempt to be either an objective journalist or a cheerleader for a particular viewpoint. Rather, he presents himself as an unapologetic, liberal-leaning, ribald, foul-mouthed, iconoclastic pundit who has specifically and thoughtfully chosen an agenda of items he wants his audience to ponder and chew on long after the show is off the air. Although stern and at times draconian in his pronouncements, his shows averages over four million viewers an episode.

But if there is one towering figure in political satire of the twenty-first century, it is Jon Stewart. One of the two most important American comedians of the twenty-first century (the other is Dave Chappelle, whom we discuss later), Stewart simultaneously revolutionized and galvanized political comedy for a post-9/11 world through his sixteen-year captaincy of *The Daily Show*. Alternating between the precise, confident wit of a ranting George Carlin, the nerdy and clever self-undermining of a Woody Allen nebbish, and the unapologetic political opinions of an Edward R. Murrow newsman, Stewart delivered serious criticism and clever jokes at a point in American political history not terribly hospitable to either.

First hosted by Craig Kilborn, *The Daily Show* was originally more a vehicle for absurdist takes on the news and pithy comments on popular culture than a platform for political commentary. In this, *The Daily Show* joined a long lineage. Going back at least to 1934, when MGM produced some "Wotaphony Newsreels" depicting events with fake comedic narration over them,[19] and continuing in the long tradition of newspapers making up fake news stories on April Fool's Day, the lighthearted humor in delivering fake news has always had its place in American culture. Stewart took over in 1999 and converted it to a show comically focused on politics and the national media, in the tradition of more pointedly satirical shows like *That Was the Week That Was* or *The Smothers Brothers Comedy Hour*.

The transition was not immediate. Stewart, though bringing a stronger political bite, still began with some of the spoofy conceits of the old format, making use of his incredibly strong stable of "correspondents," then still relatively unknown, to pull it off. The standard format for *The Daily Show* at the time (still used, though relied on less frequently, today) was Stewart playfully "reporting" on the headlines from his anchor desk before calling on various special correspondents to provide "in-depth coverage" on various hot-button news stories of the day.

Stewart's *The Daily Show* began in earnest with "Indecision 2000," the show's ongoing coverage of the 2000 presidential primaries and elections. Here's a particularly illustrative and funny moment: On the August 3, 2000, episode, the crew was covering the Republican National Convention, with Stewart at the desk and some of the correspondents reporting from the field. After taking shots at Dick Cheney's record of voting against a bill condemning the imprisonment of Nelson Mandela and at George W. Bush's capital punishment record in Texas, the show moved on to the official nomination of George W. Bush. Upon his receiving the Republican nomination, the camera showed then governor George W. Bush become, shall we say, *aroused* by the honor. Stewart had the camera show this again in slow motion, commenting, "I guess they are really the big tent party." He turned to then correspondent Steve Carrell, asking whether Bush would be successful in bringing the party to the center. Carrell, on camera from the convention floor, responded with perfect faux seriousness, "Judging by his reaction, it seems that this nominee really does lean to the right." This juvenilia continued with Stephen Colbert ("It's clear that Bush is standing tall in a recent poll") and

Nancy Walls ("The state of the union is turgid") getting in their shots until Vance DeGeneres—brother of Ellen and owner of maybe the best deadpan deliveries in comic history—delivered the closing line of the bit: "All I have to say is: welcome to the Johnson administration."[20]

The mix of serious, pointed commentary with a series of penis jokes was perfectly on-brand. However, after the United States found itself embroiled in wars in Iraq and Afghanistan, Stewart became one of the best-known and most-listened-to voices of dissent against the administration and the media apparatus that refused to hold it to account. This situation came to a head in Stewart's famous appearance on *Crossfire*, a news-banter show on CNN that featured Paul Bagala, Tucker Carlson, James Carville, and others in a "debate" between Republicans and Democrats. Stewart came on not to take on any particular side but to eviscerate the show and its participants—"partisan hacks"—for engaging in political theater while the country was being misled into war. When Carlson tried to criticize Stewart for not asking hard-hitting questions himself, Stewart responded that he was on Comedy Central, not CNN, and that "if the news organizations look to Comedy Central for their cues on integrity, we're in bad shape!" *Crossfire* was cancelled not long after Stewart's appearance.

This point was, it must be noted, a long-running criticism of Stewart: he would lob satirical grenades at his targets, but when they pushed back at him, he would claim that he was a comedian, not a news analyst or political pundit, and so the criticisms were misdirected. At times it appeared like a bit of a dodge. But his distinction is important. A comedian's responsibility is ultimately to the joke, with the insights, commentary, and political criticism being important insofar as they enable the punchlines to land. To hold him to the same standards as a real political journalist would be to conflate the satirist with the analyst—and perhaps admit how much of a joke politics had become.

On his *Crossfire* appearance, Stewart said that when it came to absurdity, it would be hard to top the Bush administration. Little did he know what would eventually come. Stewart left *The Daily Show* just before Trump won the nomination and eventually the presidency, so he never got to be the anchor for the most absurd presidency to date.

Still, Stewart had some good, prescient material on pre-presidential Trump. In 2011, after making a political name for himself by demanding that President Obama produce his long-form birth certificate to prove he was American, Trump brought Sarah Palin to New York City, where they were filmed eating "real" New York pizza in Times Square. Stewart, initially respecting the move, became outraged upon discovering that the "real" pizzeria they visited was the chain Famous Famiglia. The bit continues with Stewart getting increasingly incensed (and increasingly Italian sounding) over Trump's lack of New York pizza etiquette ("You stack your slices?" "Are you eating it with a fork? . . . Donald Trump, why don't you take that fork and stick it in New York's eye?") before concluding, "You know what, based on how you eat pizza, Donald, I want to see your long-form birth certificate: I don't think you were really born in New York." Somehow, this long riff on a relatively simple and small affair manages to be both funny and perspectival while still very astutely making a real and subtle point about the opportunism and phoniness of Trump's political persona.

In 2015, when Stewart left the show, his replacement, Trevor Noah, knew better than to tamper with success and didn't change the formula of the show (although his production crew finally made the spinning globe rotate counterclockwise, correctly!), but he has added his own very distinct and clever perspective (if you haven't seen it, go on YouTube and find Noah's take on Trump and African dictators).

In addition to Noah, *The Daily Show* has produced a long list of alumni who have gone on to be successful stand-up comics and comedic actors. To date, six of them have gone on to create their own versions of fake news programs: Stephen Colbert, Samantha Bee, Hasan Minhaj, John Oliver, Larry Wilmore, and Michelle Wolf.

(Although Wilmore's and Wolf's shows initially earned solid reviews, both were canceled.)

From 2005 to 2014, Stephen Colbert hosted *The Colbert Report* and played an over-the-top conservative reporter and pundit who was the ideological opposite of Jon Stewart and the doppelganger of Fox News's Bill O'Reilly of *The O'Reilly Factor* (1996–2017). Sitting behind his news desk, Colbert interpreted rather than reported the news of the day from an absurdly Far Right point of view. The conceit of *The Colbert Report* was that in comically advocating a right-wing conservative point of view, he was in fact lampooning and criticizing it.

John Oliver's satirical version of a news show, *Last Week Tonight* on HBO, debuted in 2014. Parodying in thirty minutes the *60 Minutes* format and covering only one story at a time in depth and detail, Oliver mockingly eviscerates the subject matter of the week. "What we do is not fake news," insists Oliver; "we are very, very sure about every piece of information that we pass along, we fact check and recheck everything."[21] The purpose of the show, said Oliver, is to use comedy as a vehicle to examine "the things I care about."[22] For example, Oliver points out that "it's a strange time [for the Trump administration] to be in love with America right now.... Falling in love with America right now is like falling in love with a girl who's throwing up all over herself. All you can do is hold her hair back and say, 'Let it all out. You just made a mistake, that's all.'"[23]

Samantha Bee had the longest run as a correspondent on *The Daily Show* until 2016, when she began to host her own show on TBS, *Full Frontal*. Unlike her two fellow alums, Bee does not sit behind a desk, and she makes no attempt to play the role of an objective, impartial news reporter. Rather, she paces back and forth across the screen and plays the role of a plucky, pissed-off pundit with a DGAF (don't give a fuck!) attitude while simultaneously wielding the twin swords of liberal progressivism and feminism.

After serving as a "special correspondent" on *The Daily Show* for four years, Hasan Minhaj was offered a thirty-two-part, half-hour, weekly show on Netflix. In an intimate theater space with a state-of-the-art screen and soundstage, and doing a spot-on impression of John Oliver on speed, Minhaj informs and preaches to an audience of millennials and postmillennials on the dire consequences of "The Corruption of Brazil's Rain Forest," "The Global Influence of the NRA," "Why the Internet Sucks!," and, even though most Americans could not care less, "Corrupt Practices in World Cricket Play!" Minhaj believes that he is successful because he is "standing on the shoulders" of a few real geniuses. As a major player in the new art form of "comedic journalism," Minhaj believes that *The*

Daily Show, its spin-offs, Bill Maher, and the recasting of Stephen Colbert from a card-carrying conservative to the "Supreme Pontiff of Democratic Liberalism" on CBS's new *Late Show* have become, for more and more people, the "current equivalent of journalism." That is, it is the place people look to for both basic information and political commentary.[24] In other words, says Minhaj, the "new comedic journalism" has become America's new "marketplace of ideas." Facts, fiction, and fun are intermixed on these shows, and it's left to the audience to distinguish one from the others.[25]

According to Peter Sagal, host of NPR's *Wait Wait... Don't Tell Me!* (a comedy show that asks "silly fake questions" about "real news items"), audiences have become accustomed to and are comfortable with the format of "fake news shows." Viewers understand that the purpose of these shows is to be "out of the box" and irreverent with regard to news and information. Overall, Sagal suggests that audiences now recognize that the goal of these shows is to be funny and entertaining, but at the same time they do offer their audiences information and analysis that makes them a little more aware of the political nuances of a particular situation. For Sagal, there is a kind of honesty, objectivity, and neutrality in this awareness. Audiences know how and are able to discern fact from fiction. They can enjoy the joke, and then they are left to decide for themselves regarding the issues beyond the jokes.[26] Although laughter makes reality perhaps more accessible and bearable, Sagal very much doubts whether anyone says after watching a John Oliver bit, "Oh, I just heard this joke, and I'm not a Democrat, or Republican, or a vegetarian anymore!" Audiences get the jokes and are also able to discern the political nuances and information contained within the jokes.[27]

Adam Gopnik of the *New Yorker* has suggested that reason is not always the language of life or politics, and trying to apply reasons where reason doesn't exist doesn't work.[28] Often, we need to address the matters of life from a slightly skewed point of view. "Sometimes," said Mel Brooks, "the only response to the absurdity of life and politics is to laugh at it."[29]

Although political satire is a distinct kind of humor, we are convinced that political satirists live out the central thesis of this book. Humor, joke telling, and political satire make life less opaque, more bearable, and more interesting. Jokes offer us, if only temporarily, a different geography of life, a different focus on reality. Satirical humor, like jokes, can offer us a moment of delight and a break from our fears, a reprieve, a distraction, a temporary escape from absurdity. In the words of theologian Reinhold Niebuhr, "Meeting the disappointments and frustrations of life, the irrationalities and contingencies with laughter, is a high form of wisdom."[30]

Chapter 2

The Satirical Imperative

"Satire is simultaneously funny, offensive, foolish, a farce, a contradiction, a weapon, an art form, a mystery, and a gift. We're lucky to have it!"

—Ronald M. Green

Although modesty is not one of our key virtues, we need to begin with a disclaimer. We are not scholars of literary criticism. Nor are we students of epistemology, etymology, or lexicology . . . thank God! We are, however, long-time students and lovers of comedy. The purpose of this project is to examine the role and importance of humor, joke telling, and especially satire in our private and public lives.

We are not, however, out to itemize, examine, and debate all of the vagaries and nuances of satire. Nor are we out to take on and critique the titans in the field, such as Horace, Juvenal, Aristophanes, Lucian, Chaucer, Pope, Voltaire, and Swift or more modern luminaries such as Northrop Frye and Matthew Hudgart. Rather, we want to come up with a working definition of satire and examine its role as a buffer, a tool, and a weapon against the absurdities of our political world.

Joke telling and satire are joined at the hip. Both are an attempt to alleviate and possibly elevate the human condition. The great Mel Brooks believes that we need humor, we need jokes in our lives, because otherwise our "collective lamentations" about the trials and tribulations of the world would be unbearable. We all need jokes, says Brooks, as a "defense against the universe."[1] Humor allows us to fight off the fears that living a human life inevitably brings. Humor can keep us at a distance from our fear of the confusing, the unknown, the unanswerable, and the unacceptable. As novelist Philip Kerr succinctly put it, "Laughter conceals a scream against life!"[2]

Following Brooks's and Kerr's leads, we want to argue that joke telling and satire are means of dealing with the everyday problems of life as well as many of the more elusive and mysterious questions of existence. Jokes are weapons made of words, acting as both sword and shield to defend and protect us against life.[3] They allow us to take on taboos, poke fun at life, and mock human frailty. Humor can, at times, illuminate (if not completely explain) some of the irresoluble problems and mysteries that all of us face. And, if all else fails, humor and satire at least can hold off and fight off our fear of the unanswerable and the unacceptable.

During his last week hosting *The Daily Show*, Jon Stewart elegantly encapsulated the time-honored role and purpose of jesters, fools, satirists, comics, and joke telling: "Jokes are a narrative that helps us negotiate reality." In other words, humor makes life bearable.[4]

Joke telling and satire are, at the very least, a pleasant distraction. They are a timeout. They offer a moment of reprieve. They are a safety valve. They (temporarily) can disarm a moment. When we laugh at one of life's mysteries, cruelties, or horrors, we diminish—if only temporarily—its terror in our imagination. Jokes and satire offer us a window into the unknowable and irresolvable. Jokes about sex, marriage, children, money, illness, death, religion, and God may not provide definitive answers, but they can alleviate some of our fears, afford comfort and distraction, and perhaps, just perhaps, offer us some perspective, some illumination in regard to these fundamentally irresolvable and yet unavoidable issues. Jokes, humor, and satire allow us to face reality and, for a moment, not be defeated by it. And, lest we forget, jokes are also simply fun. Poet and comedy connoisseur Andrew Hudgins argues that, as a species, we love to joke and "need to laugh" because there is a "punctuating power to humor."[5] Whatever function humor might serve, there is something, at root, deeply *human* about the ability to laugh and the desire to hear others laugh.

Sharing a joke with someone, not unlike breaking bread, helps affirm a shared human experience and urge. An optimist might say that whatever else a joke is, it is first and foremost a reminder of what joys life can entail.

Of course, we're not all optimists. Friedrich Nietzsche, the German philosopher (who, take our word for it, did not have a particularly sunny disposition), had a different take. Freddy "Handlebars" Nietzsche suggested that gazing too long into the "gaping abyss" of the unanswerable and unfathomable issues and questions of life leads to despair and futility.[6]

But there is a middle ground between the optimist and the gaping abyss. French philosopher André Comte-Sponville (are there any French philosophers who are funny?) argues that humor is a kind of mourning and mocking of the human condition. Humor accepts the human condition as sad and scary and then talks about it, pokes fun at it, laughs at it, and laughs at our feeble responses to it. In so doing, it frees us from dread. It softens the blow of reality.[7] We want to argue that laughter, satire, and joke telling are a way to gaze into the abyss, confront the unknowable, and perhaps find comfort and perspective even if no absolute answers are to be found. It allows us to be realistic about the limits of our own knowledge while also finding joy and community in the process.

To joke—to satirically take jabs at topics such as illness, death, God, sex, and age—is a way of defanging or domesticating something that essentially cannot be tamed. It is a means of taking charge of something that we really cannot control or completely understand. Joking about a "deep topic" or "dangerous topic" is a way of talking about it, examining it in a way that doesn't scare us, numb us, and rob us of our joy in life.[8] Jokes allow us to dwell on the incomprehensible without dying from fear or going mad. As the great American philosopher Joan Rivers succinctly stated, "If you can laugh at it, you can live with it."[9] At least for a while!

According to the onetime "King of Comedy" Jerry Seinfeld, good jokes may not be the same as full-blown philosophical arguments or disputations, but they are critically important with regard to the state of our mental health. Seinfeld believes that jokes are "precious material" and a "gift" we give to each other. "People tell jokes," says Seinfeld, "by the score, because what else are you going to do to maintain sanity?"[10] For Seinfeld, big jokes (marriage, death, religion) or little jokes (check-writing etiquette, cell phone protocol, five-hour energy drinks) are little playlets that are funny (or not) depending on word play, timing, and delivery. Jokes are limited vignettes, not definitive dissertations. Comedy, for Seinfeld, is about observing and playfully appreciating the difficulties and incongruities of life. As he succinctly put it, "Comedy gives you a moment of weightlessness. It relieves you of the weight of your problems."[11] Comedy can temporarily disarm and displace the pain and tribulations of life. Comedy offers comfort and not a cure. It offers diversion and not closure. It is an expedient and not a remedy. As essayist Christopher Buckley succinctly put it, humor, like alcohol, at least makes our problems and other people momentarily less troublesome.[12]

Because one of the purposes of jokes is to help us deal with our very real and often painful lives, jokes change, evolve, contract, expand, and/or recede to match the times we live in and the topics, personalities, and issues that occupy our lives. Comedy must absorb, mimic, and/or respond to the happenings of the moment, which is why it is one of the most malleable art forms. Comedy is a creature of its surroundings. You don't get drunk jokes unless there are drunks. Gladiator jokes didn't get started until they were butchering each other in the Roman Colosseum. No one satirized "the Kardashians" until the Kardashians showed up on the celebrity scene and became "the Kardashians." The same holds true for jokes about Pope Francis, Lady Gaga, Bernie Madoff (Wait, he wasn't funny! And what he did was no laughing matter!), the NFL, rednecks, Starbucks, and the sitting president—whoever he or she may be. (By the way, according to a number of historians, J. Q. Adams, Martin Van Buren, James Polk, James Buchanan, and Chester A. Arthur were not funny, had no sense of humor, and never told jokes. Which, come to think of it, is sort of funny and sad.)

Satire provides a different sort of comfort than other kinds of humor. Tellers of satire (satirists or *satiristas*, as comedy writer Paul Provenza refers to them) are comics with an edge. They do not just tell jokes; they don't use comedy to offer comfort or relief. Rather, they use comedy to challenge, critique, and confront the world. Satirists are contrarians or comic critics who intentionally set out to belittle, debunk, and/or deconstruct the social and political status quo.[13] Satire is both in the business of entertainment and in the service of change, renewal, and reform. According to journalist and raconteur extraordinaire James Geary, satire simultaneously attempts to entertain, enlighten, and engage.[14]

At its core, satire is different from just telling innocuous jokes and clever stories. Satire, somewhat like sarcasm (from the Greek word *sarkazein*—"to rend the flesh, to chew the lips in rage"), is the use of taunting, sneering, or cutting remarks in an attempt to annoy, make sense of, denounce, or deride a perceived folly or vice. Satirical comments/jokes can simultaneously be funny and prickly, annoying, and offensive. Our best satirists can be vicious, with their humor only available to us in hindsight.

The thesis behind all satire is that "the human condition is inherently flawed and deserving of ridicule and verbal abuse."[15] Satirists seek out the absurdity in everything. They see life generally, and politics specifically, as worthy of rage and mockery. Nothing is above reproach.

Satirists do not calmly preach. They rant! They screech! Satirists act as the "town criers" who use trenchant wit to expose and discredit absurdity, excess, vice, and folly. Satirists seek to examine and excoriate the world around them. Whether calm or agitated in their demeanor and presence, satirists are by nature irreverent and subversive. They are by disposition simultaneously curious, skeptical, and cynical about the world around them. To paraphrase English essayist John Dryden, satirists are the physicians of society. The true end of satire is to cure and correct corruption and vice.[16]

Satirists use humor to "puncture pomposity"[17] and critique the status quo. They are not policy advocates, arguing for some solution. If they were, they wouldn't be funny—they'd be preachy. Satirists are funniest when they are resisting the seduction of easy answers and self-assuredness. But this doesn't mean satire is inherently nihilistic. Even if no cure or resolution is possible, satirists at least raise the question "Can we do better?" Robert Mankoff, cartoon editor for the *New Yorker*, argues that "political satire is ridicule dedicated to exposing the difference between appearance and reality in the public life." The justification for this mockery "is that by holding bad behavior up to ridicule, we might (possibly) laugh folly out of existence."[18]

However, it is important to keep in mind that the ultimate purpose of satire is not always a negative act or judgment. In its broadest sense, satire is an examination and a "critique" of the status quo. To "critique" does not always mean to completely and utterly deconstruct or destroy. To "critique" also means to examine, to take apart, to understand, to correct, to put back together again, to make better. In its most positive light, satire is a blend of "ridicule and affection," with the latter often being the dominant and preferred objective.[19] That is, satire uses ridicule to rectify: in highlighting and ridiculing the foibles, incompetence, or corruption of social practices, political leaders, or government actions, satire seeks to understand their behavior so that we might come up with a remedy for their folly.[20]

In *Anatomy of Criticism* (1957), Northrop Frye defines satire as "militant irony." We prefer a somewhat less elegant but perhaps more accurate phrase: "militant contrarianism." Satirists are combative contrarians. They are aroused and angry and aggressively seek confrontation and correction. Satirists use caustic comic commentary to highlight and often ironically show up the foibles and falsehoods of the proposition or situation at hand. Satirists use humor in an attempt to denounce, degrade, and deride those conditions and situations we accept without reflection. Different from joke tellers and entertainers who simply seek a humorous and playful appreciation of the difficulties and incongruities of life, satirists seek to directly confront the uncomfortable and unavoidable vexations of life.

Satirists respond to the world with a mixture of laughter and indignation. Initially expressed as entertainment, all satire contains elements of contempt, critique, attack, and transformation. Satirists see both the flawed world we live in and the better world we desire.[21] To borrow a line from Jonathan Swift, satirists seek to "mend the world as far as they are able."[22] What distinguishes satire from other kinds of writing, whether the prevailing tone is comic or serious, is the moral purpose of the satirist: the desire to improve the world.

The classic example of this concept, of course, is Jonathan Swift's 1729 "Modest Proposal," an anonymously published pamphlet of just over three thousand words. He wrote it to draw attention to the linked problems of rural poverty and overpopulation in Ireland. His solution to the problem was both elegant and unusual: "Have parents sell excess children to the wealthy for food!"

It is a melancholy Object to those, who walk through this great Town or travel in the Country, when they see the Streets, the Roads and Cabbin-doors crowded with Beggars of the Female Sex, followed by three, four, or six Children, all in Rags, and importuning every Passenger for an Alms. These Mothers instead of being able to work for their honest livelihood, are forced to employ all their time in Strolling to beg Sustenance for their helpless Infants. . . . I shall now therefore humbly propose my own Thoughts, which I hope will not be liable to the least Objection.

I have been assured by a very knowing American of my acquaintance in London, that a young healthy Child well Nursed is at a year Old a most delicious, nourishing and wholesome Food, whether Stewed, Roasted, Baked, or Boiled; and I make no doubt that it will equally serve in a Fricasie or Ragoust. . . .

I can think of no one Objection, that will be possibly be raised against this Proposal, unless it should be urged, that the Number of People will be thereby much lessened in the Kingdom. This I freely own, and 'twas indeed one principal Design in offering it to the world.

The beauty of Swift's satire here is that he doesn't need to say, "The poverty in Ireland is a moral travesty." By seriously, technically, and seemingly earnestly calling for the absurd—for Irish parents to sell their young—he invites us to recognize that which we already know: a humanitarian crisis exists, and English inaction is a moral travesty.

A modern example of the classic act of "militant contrarianism" is Stephen Colbert's "countercultural denunciation" of civil rights legend Rosa Parks. He delivers his diatribe against Parks in his assumed guise as a Far Right conservative news commentator (think Bill O'Reilly, formerly of Fox News) on his old "fake Far Right wing" nightly news cast, *The Colbert Report* (2005–2014):

Rosa Parks is overrated. Let's not forget she got famous for breaking the law, okay? Last time I checked, we don't honor lawbreakers. I think that gets lost in this whole back-of-the-bus thing. Don't get me wrong, it took a lot of courage, but I think we're burying the lead, here. She's a criminal![23]

Comedian Elaine May says that satire is "comic revenge." It's the attempt to be funny, yet caustic, accusatory, and corrective. Mike Nichols, her comedic partner in crime, completely agrees. Satire is a "place to vent our rage by making as much fun as possible of those who've made us mad."[24]

On the American scene, there are many shining stars in the crowded firmament of satire and political comedy. Indeed, the American experience begins with a satirical barb by John Hancock. He famously explained that he signed his name so large on the Declaration of Independence that King George wouldn't need his glasses to read it! When we focus on professional humorists, there are, we think, at least five supernovas who are useful for thinking about the American tradition of satire: Mark Twain (1835–1910), Will Rogers (1879–1935), Mort Sahl

(1927–), Lenny Bruce (1925–1966), and George Carlin (1937–2008).

According to Ernest Hemingway, there would be no tradition of American literature without Mark Twain. Twain not only created a narrative portrait of the American experience but also used his celebrity status as a novelist and literary guru to pontificate on the pulse and politics of American life. In so doing, Twain arguably invented a characteristically *American* brand of satire. In contrast to the droll deadpan of Swift, Twain's satire reflected what Paul Schmidt once referred to as "a burlesque of the genteel tradition,"[25] sending up the convention and pretensions of the upper, learned gentry through the perspectives and insights of the unlearned "rube." By using the language and sensibilities of those thought to be "crude" to ridicule and transcend those thought to be "refined," Twain helped popularize the most enduring aspect of American satire: showing the ingenuity and insight of those thought to be imperceptive by virtue of their marginality.

Although not a stand-up comic by training, later in life, finding himself in need of work and money, Twain became a "speaker for hire," and, according to the critics of the time, he was a "gifted raconteur, distinctive humorist, and irascible moralist." According to one Twain commentator, "He never was in front of an audience that he didn't try to win over—to his personal, political, and social point of view—with laughter and charm. He relished the role of orator and comic sage, and he worked hard at it."[26] Even his one-liners were thoughtfully crafted and surgically incisive. For example, "There is no distinctive American criminal class, except Congress." Or "Reader, suppose you were an idiot, and suppose you were a member of Congress, but I repeat myself."[27]

Will Rogers was arguably America's first stand-up political satirist. In fact, he did it all. He began his career as a rodeo performer; then he moved on to vaudeville. Later, he jumped to Broadway and the "Ziegfied Follies." He also had the most-listened-to national radio show on Sunday nights, and an estimated forty million people read his biweekly column in the *New York Times*. He also wrote six books, made seventy-one movies, and, in fact, was the second-highest-grossing American movie star of his era behind the child performer Shirley Temple.

Born in Oklahoma, Rogers became America's "Cowboy Philosopher." His vaudeville act, like his radio show, was simplicity itself. He stood in front of a microphone the size of a dinner plate and talked in an easy manner about the issues of the day. He never played the role of the clown, the pundit, or the scholar. As he famously said again and again, "All I know is what I read in the papers." Rogers told jokes, but more often than not he simply delivered folksy monologues and ruminated on the issues facing the common man.[28]

Of course, the joke about Rogers was his denial that he was a true jokester or even a professional comedian. "Most actors on the stage," he said, "have some writer write their material. I don't do that. Congress is good enough for me. They have been writing my material for years." So, he concluded, "there's no trick to being a humorist when you have the whole government working for you."[29] According to Rogers, he didn't make jokes; he just reported the facts. During the Great Depression, he voiced the despair of countless individuals and families who were out of work and facing hard times.

In our estimation, the comedian who was able to incorporate Rogers's folksy delivery technique and Twain's wit and satirical barbs was Mort Sahl. In 1960, *Time* magazine dubbed him the "patriarch of a new school of comedians."[30] Sahl walked out onstage in his trademark V-neck sweater with a newspaper under his arm and casually started musing about his take on politics, politicians, social trends, and changing cultural and sexual mores. He never told salacious or grossly obscene stories. He never swore or used profane language. As one review put it, "He was both Mr. Cool and Mr. Clean."[31] He didn't deliver punchlines; he delivered observations, paradoxical and otherwise, on issues of the day. For example, "I'm for capital punishment. You've got to execute people. How else are they going to learn?" The *San Francisco Examiner* said Sahl was "funny without being very funny."[32] His jokes were wry, witty observations, syntactical word games that were humorous, if not exactly hilarious. For example, here's a joke that predates modern hipster gentrification by nearly half a century: "A yuppie [young urban professional] is someone who believes that it's courageous to eat in a restaurant that hasn't been reviewed yet!" In a tribute to Sahl in 2007, comedian Albert Brooks said that "every comedian who is not doing wife jokes has [Sahl] to thank for that. He was really the first . . . in terms of talking about stuff, not just doing punch lines."[33]

Although Mort Sahl never achieved the "superstar" fame of some of his contemporaries, his iconoclastic intellectual irreverence and sophisticated political IQ changed the nature of social commentary and satire. His performance onstage established the precedent that "standup comedy could be hip, personal, politically provocative, and psychosocially subtle."[34] Ironically, in 1959, a year before it labeled Sahl the "premier American humorist and satirist," *Time* reported being appalled by his constant comedic negativism and nihilism. It even dubbed Sahl the "original sick-nic comedian" and leader of a pack of "satirical sickies," mistakenly including Shelly Berman, Jonathan Winters, Mike Nichols and Elaine May, Don Adams, Tom Lehren, and Lenny Bruce in his posse of "sick-nics." *Time* was wrong about all of them except Lenny Bruce, who went on to both embrace and promulgate "sicknic comedy" and became its chief advocate and "true king."[35]

It can be argued that Lenny Bruce really had two careers. The first was as an aspiring comedian—who, basically, joked about the usual menu of topics that other comics served up to their respective audiences. But unlike those of Henny Youngman ("Take my wife . . . please!) or Milton Berle ("My wife and I were happy for thirty years. Then we met!"), Bruce's jokes were edgy, probing, truer to life, and more than a little uncomfortable: "Never tell . . . In fact, if your old lady walks in on you [while you . . . !], deny it. Yeah. Just flat out deny it and she'll believe it: 'I'm tellin' ya. This chick came downstairs with a sign around her neck "Lay on Top of Me or I'll Die." I didn't know what else I was gonna do . . .'" Early on in his career, even with material that pushed the usual conventional boundaries, he wasn't yet the Lenny Bruce who challenged the limits of "free speech" and obscenity standards. He was still trying to make it and win over "hip" but essentially conventional audiences. Bruce's second career as a "true iconoclast," a "shockjock," was really an extension and expansion of career one . . . but now fueled by drugs.

Bruce claimed that comedians in older generations "were doing an act." They were in show business. They weren't concerned with the truth; they just wanted to be funny and make people laugh. But Bruce argued that he was not doing an act; he was telling the truth. He said all of his humor was based on his outrage and despair with regard to the state of the world. According to Lewis Black, "Lenny confronted and challenged his audience with hard, dark truths wrapped in twisted scenarios of his own invention!" Bruce, said Black, was looking for laughs where no one had looked before. And in getting his audience to laugh, perhaps he also got them to look at a different understanding of the "truth" of things.[36]

As Bruce evolved from popular comedian to nightclub Cassandra, sharing news of impending chaos, gloom, and doom with his audience, his tone and demeanor became more aggressive and assertive, his language and punchlines more salacious, and his open use of "controlled substances" made him an easy target for law enforcement. Between 1959 and his death in August 1966, he was busted for drugs, arrested and fined for obscenity, or barred from performing in various venues both in America and abroad at least twelve different times.[37] As his popularity, notoriety, and legal difficulties grew, Bruce outed himself. "I'm not a comedian. I'm not sick. The world is sick and I'm the doctor. I am a satirist, basically," he said. "I am irreverent politically, religiously, on anything I think needs discussing and satirizing." Late in his career, after doing a show in San Francisco, he was arrested for obscenity. His only comment: "I wasn't very funny tonight . . . sometimes I'm not. I'm not a comedian.

I'm Lenny Bruce."[38] Nonetheless, a lot of people say that he was both—a comedian and a satirist—especially one of his biggest fans: George Carlin.

It can also be argued that George Carlin, like his idol and role model, Lenny Bruce, had two distinct phases to his comedic career. The first part of his career started with his attempt to be funny between "spinning platters" as a disk jockey. For a while he did both radio and stand-up with a partner (Jack Burns). He told jokes; he did shtick. He also did impersonations of celebrities and politicians. Reportedly, he did a spot-on uptight, leering Richard Nixon. And he did a parody of John Fitzgerald Kennedy that infuriated the latter's father, Joseph Kennedy. Clean shaven and dressed in a suit and tie, his hair heavily slicked down with Brylcreem, Carlin played Al Sleet, "the hippy dippy weatherman: Tonight's forecast: dark!" He also imitated the newscast style of award-winning TV journalists Chet Huntley and David Brinkley and reported on the nightly "fake news" of the day.

Tonight, the world breathes a little easier, as five more nations have signed the "Nuclear Test Ban Treaty." Today's signers were Chad, Sierra Leone, Upper Volta, Morocco, and Iceland . . . Quickly now, the basketball scores.—110 to 102 and 125 to 113. And there was one overtime duel, 99–98. Oh, and here's a partial score: 14–12.

Sometime around 1970, Carlin no longer felt like he fit the comic mold of TV variety shows, even one as culturally edgy as *The Smothers Brothers Comedy Hour*. Nor did he want to do one-liners like Myron Cohen and Jack E. Leonard. He didn't want to do bits. He wanted to say his own words. He wanted to be more like his role model and idol, Lenny Bruce. He came to the realization that comics should have something to say and not simply tell jokes. And so he decided to stop being mainstream.

Step one in the process: Start using and abusing some serious drugs! Step two: Stop shaving and grow a ponytail. Step three: Stop dressing like a dutiful middle-manager type. Step four: Assume the role of comedic gadfly and happy sage. Step five: Make fun of the "little" things of the world—food, pets, work, and relationships. Step six: Make fun of the "big" stuff—war, politics, death, social issues. Step seven: Become America's chief First Amendment advocate and ask why, of the four hundred thousand–plus words in the English language, just seven of them are thought to be too dirty and improper for use on public airwaves. (In case you've forgotten, they are "shit, piss, fuck, cunt, cocksucker, motherfucker, and tits!"[39])

Ironically, George Carlin did not think of himself as a "classical satirist." He wasn't necessarily interested in converting his audience or correcting the situation he was making fun of. He said he was doing it because what he wanted to say was true and funny. As he insisted a number of times, "I frankly don't give a fuck how it all turns out in this country—or anywhere else for that matter!"[40] Whether we label him a satirist, a nihilist, a contrarian, or simply a curmudgeon, George Carlin perceived the world from a skewed perspective, and he took great delight in making fun of it and us.

According to comedy historian Kliph Nesteroff, the 1950s were when "comedy changed forever, for the better!"[41] Mort Sahl "instigated a paradigm shift" and revolutionized stand-up comedy and satire for new generations to come. Mort Sahl led to Lenny Bruce, and Bruce then led to George Carlin. From these three have come a cascade of faces and names, now synonymous with contemporary comedy, who have forever altered the comedic, satiric landscape.

CHAPTER 3

Satirical Animals

"God bless our good and gracious King,
Whose promise we now rely on,
Who never said a foolish thing,
Nor even did a wise one."
—THE EARL OF ROCHESTER ON KING CHARLES II

Political humor and satire are, perhaps, as old as comedy itself. It's possible that right after some unknown Egyptian comic made fun of the constantly fluctuating depth of the Nile, the peculiar shape of the pyramids, or the discomfort of ancient headdresses, he or she took a cheap shot at the pharaoh and his mummy and daddy issues! In the last chapter we looked at how satire helps us personally. Here, we're going to be a bit more argumentative. We want to claim that satire, particularly political satire—"speaking truth to power," poking fun at the extremes and absurdities of social and cultural conventions—is crucial to our society and our collective sense of self.

If there is anything like a thesis to our book, it is what we say in this chapter: satire isn't just something we do in response to politics, but something basic to the types of beings we are. We think that the comedic tradition does not start with sex jokes, blonde jokes, drunk jokes, ethnic jokes, fart jokes, or whatever. Rather, our propensity for humor, our joke-telling ability, came out of our need to push back against the trials and tribulations of life and to make fun of society and the everyday norms of the world around us. If the ability to laugh is a natural human trait, one of the most natural things for us to laugh at is the way we interact with others and the way power structures our lives.

Why would this be the case? Why would "society" be a more natural target of comedy than, say, sex, flatulence, or booze? For one, it's because sex, booze, ethnicity, and anything else you might want to joke about are *always* infused with politics. How we have sex, whom we have sex with, what we drink, what we eat, and who seems like "an outsider" aren't purely natural but always shaped by social expectation and sanction. Researcher Ken Jennings has argued that "all comedy is political." We agree. If "everything is political," as political science students like to remind everyone, then every joke is, in a certain sense, a political joke.

For instance, historians who study this sort of thing say that the oldest recorded joke dates back to 1900 BCE. Translated from ancient Sumerian, the old zinger goes like this: "Something which has never occurred since time immemorial [has happened]: a young woman did not fart in her husband's lap!"[1] OK, so maybe it's not a terribly good joke, but it's clearly a joke. In fact, at first glance it seems like an early example of a very recognizable sort of joke that we still tell today—the fart joke. One might read this jest and infer that our oldest form of humor is toilet humor.

But it's actually more than a fart joke. Let's think about it a bit more. It's not just about a random, contextless person farting. It's not one friend turning to the other and saying "Pull my finger" in Sumerian. There are specific, familiar social roles involved—namely, a husband and a young bride. There is also a familiar situation—an intimate scene of a couple cuddling.

And then the wife cuts or does not cut the Mesopotamian cheese! Here's the political point. She's the wife! Wives have special prerogatives. Husbands may be mates, protectors, potential fathers of children—but, politically, women are in charge, and if they want to fart on their husbands' lap to signal their power and prerogatives inside the marriage, so be it!

It's more than just a fart joke. Like a Joan Rivers bit or a Dave Chappelle sketch, it's a send-up of the familiar social conventions and power structures of the day. We know the relationship and the situation—indeed, the joke presents it as something so familiar that it has existed from time immemorial. It is a "state of the fart" joke. (Authors' note: Sorry for that, we couldn't let that one . . . pass!) In farting, or not, we might say the ancient Sumerian wife is *relieving the pressure* created by social expectations.

And isn't that what satire is all about? Disrupting the conventional and taken-for-granted with the ridiculous and silly? Indeed, it's about showing how ridiculous and silly what we take for granted is! Satire is confrontational. It's about pushback, dissent, discord, disappointment, and demonstrating the absurdity of the status quo. While not exactly "high art," a well-timed fart can certainly lead us to recognize how much our conventions stink.

But it goes even deeper than that. It's not just that almost everything we care about is shaped by politics. It's that humans, as Aristotle once famously said, are "political animals" (*zoon politikon*).[2] This is a term that gets thrown out a lot, but it's worth spelling out exactly what Aristotle meant.

Why would politics be so important? According to Aristotle, it is because only in political society can we ever fully cultivate and perfect our innate human capacities. One of the great human abilities is our capacity for *logos*, or reasoned speech. Many living creatures can communicate: bees can tell other bees where pollen is through dance, and dogs can establish hierarchies by sniffing each other's rear ends. But humans are different (although maybe we're not that different from dogs in how we establish order). What humans appear uniquely capable of is the ability to engage in rational argument. Monkeys can yell and holler when a predator is near, but humans have the unique ability to debate what counts as a predator and the best way to respond to one.

Aristotle, therefore, thought one of the highest human activities was cultivating this ability to reason. A human life in which we never practice and grow this capacity is a human life not fully lived. Man is a "political animal," according to Aristotle, because it is only in political communities that we can fully cultivate this capability. Why? First of all, because political communities allow us to create surpluses, which give us the resources and time to stop working and start debating. More important, political community creates the *need* for rational argument. Politics always brings us face-to-face with difference: people with different backgrounds, with different positions in society, and different ideas of what we should do. To live in a political society is to be repeatedly confronted with people with whom you radically disagree but with whom you must still live and cooperate. And so we are forced to argue, to debate—to use our rational capacities. And through that use, we perfect and strengthen it.

"Man is a political animal," then, because we need political community to flourish and live good lives. Aristotle warns that those who are unable or unwilling to live in the polis must be a beast or a god, but not properly human. And yet the best-laid plans of mice and Greeks can and do go awry (to paraphrase a great Scottish poet and satirist). That politics *can* enable us to flourish doesn't mean it always does. As we all know, politics is a theater for spectacular folly, corruption, and stupidity more often than it is a stage for human virtue. As Robin Williams once quipped, politics has an interesting etymology: "Politics: 'Poli,' a Latin word meaning 'many'; and 'tics' meaning 'bloodsucking creatures.'"[3] Even if political life is something that can allow us to be our best selves, politics always, even at its best, comes with annoyances, encumbrances, and absurdities, as anyone who has ever been to the DMV can attest. At worst, politics brings with it injustice, rancor, bigotry, and violence. Even as we naturally gravitate toward it, politics always entails conventions, institutions, and behaviors that strike us as wrong or that don't make any sense. Like a moth to a burning candle, we are attracted to the idea of a collective political life and inevitably find ourselves burned by the reality.

Satire is our response to this inescapable fact of the human condition. We need politics, but we also can't help but notice how awful it all is. And so what do we do? We laugh at it! Aristotle almost got it right. Man is, by nature, a *satirical* animal. We naturally need political and social structures and cultures to shape our lives. And we inevitably find ourselves underwhelmed by them. Satire is unavoidable: we can't help but laugh at the irony in this.

But this isn't all! In laughing at our futile political worlds, we also can come to see what we have in *common*. Satire doesn't just mock—it can connect us by showing how, underneath all our superficial differences, we all recognize the absurdity of political life and that we all share that other natural human capacity—the capacity to laugh together. In making us laugh at our political worlds, satire can contribute to our commitment to making these worlds better and to correcting immoral or unjust facts.

However, we don't mean that satire helps us by advocating good policies, spreading awareness, or getting better people elected. It might do this too—many people credit Hannibal Buress's jokes about Bill Cosby with being a big reason why he was brought to justice for his crimes.[4] But this isn't necessarily satire's forte. We've all seen comedians who stop joking and start preaching, and though we might smile and nod, we also roll our eyes a bit: "OK, yes, you are a very righteous and good person. Now make with the funny." The point of satire generally isn't to provide a solution but to recognize how ridiculous the problem is! This is the biggest difference between preachers and satirists: the former think they have an answer to a social question, while the latter know that any answer is just a setup for another punchline.

In the twenty-first century there is no better example of this facet of satire than Dave Chappelle. Chappelle's humor involves unflinching honesty about race and racial relations in the United States. But he avoids preacherly didactics, preferring instead absurdism, character work, and juvenile humor. The result is comedy that levels deep criticisms at American society without dismissing the American experiment and still holding out some hope of redeeming it. Chappelle's satire preserves the promise of political life while demonstrating its illogic, unfairness, and stupidity.

Chappelle began his game-altering and career-making special *Killin' Them Softly*—filmed in Washington, DC, not far from his native Silver Spring, Maryland—with an observation: "DC has changed. It's different now." He waits two beats and then delivers the rest: "Lotta white folk walkin' around!" He continues, over the roaring, largely black crowd, "It was not like this in the '80s. When crack was going on. . . . Remember when crack was going on? White people were looking at DC from Virginia with binoculars." Here he switches to his trademark white guy voice: "Well, that looks dangerous. Not yet!"[5] There's an entire commentary on race relations, gentrification, the fallout from the war on drugs, and community, all in those six words delivered in the voice of a corny white guy.

Before this point, Chappelle was known but not the famous comedian he is today. Prior to *Killin' Them Softly*, he had been touring comedy clubs for years and making small appearances in various TV shows and movies. This included a 1995 cameo on *Home Improvement* with Jim Breuer (which resulted in a short-lived ABC sitcom called *Buddies*, cancelled after a month), a small part in Mel Brooks's *Robin Hood: Men in Tights* (as the Moorish Achoo, son of Asneeze, played by Isaac Hayes), and a role as Tom Hanks's colleague and token black friend in Nora Ephron's *You've Got Mail* ("Don't you feel bad, sending this broke white lady back to the projects?" he asks Hanks, referring to Meg Ryan's character). More notably, Chappelle made waves in his small but memorable role as the offensively bad lounge comedian in *The Nutty Professor*, whose big tagline—"Women be shoppin'"—has become cultural shorthand for a bad comedian with a hackneyed, sexist schtick. He also starred in and co-wrote (with longtime friend and comedy partner Neal Brennan) *Half Baked*, a stoner flick that bombed in the theaters but became a cult classic among a certain hazy-eyed set.

All of which is to say, Chappelle wasn't exactly unknown before he did his famous white guy voice, talking about the gentrification of Washington, DC. But that special, and the jokes that followed, made him into arguably the most important American comedian of the twenty-first century. Largely on the strength of that special, Chappelle launched his groundbreaking sketch show *Chappelle's Show*. Chappelle later noted that sketch comedy was not a medium he was partial to, and indeed the best routines work because they are more like visually rendered stand-up bits then sketch comedy per se. The various characters and scenarios that populate his sketches all play because they caricature familiar figures, bringing them out to the extremes to point at the absurdities of American race relations.

Chappelle drew on two important influences. The first, which he has stated explicitly was important for his comedic development, was Bugs Bunny.[6] This might seem odd at first, but if you think about his spastic facial expressions, his fourth-wall-breaking knowing smiles to the audience, and his various voices, it becomes obvious. Bugs Bunny, it should be noted, was always a satirical thumb-in-the-nose at American culture. The wise-cracking rabbit, with a history going back to West Africa,[7] who spoke in an amalgam of Bronx and Brooklyn accents,[8] was a stand-in for regular people who see through the stupidity of the powerful. Bugs always got the best of his enemies, even if he was generally dropping anvils instead of philosophical insights.

Chappelle's second influence is, of course, Richard Pryor. Pryor's influence on American comedy is second to none and perhaps matched only by that of Mark Twain himself. The Chicago-based Museum of Broadcast Communication referred to Pryor's contribution as "revolutionary humor," creating characters drawn from archetypes of the lived black experience in order to "ridicule and comment upon the circumstances under which African Americans live."[9] One of Pryor's most memorable characters was Mudbone, an old wino from Pryor's hometown of Peoria, Illinois, whom he would inhabit onstage for long stretches of time, telling stories and jokes from this perspective. The character was created in one week at the LA comedy institution the Comedy Store.[10] These monologues would often meander through various topics and digressions, making the audience laugh (sometimes uncomfortably) through Mudbone's caustic, yet unpretentious, observations. These characters garnered Pryor comparisons with Twain, as the torchbearer of American satire, by Bob Newhart: "Mark Twain wrote about life on the frontier, what it was like growing up on the Mississippi River, and Richard Pryor tells what it was like growing up in the inner city,"[11] bringing out both the humor and trenchant observations of mainstream society that such a perspective allows.

Clayton Bigsby, the black white supremacist, or Tyrone Biggums, Chappelle's go-to dusty crackhead, are only the easiest and most straightforward examples of how Chappelle took Pryor's genius and Bugs Bunny's spastic humor to develop characters who shoved the reality of American race relations in our faces and, by getting us to laugh at it, kept us from looking away. We'd recap the sketches here, but, frankly, just as one should not make graven images of the almighty, one ought not besmirch such comedy gold by trying to render it in print.

The rawness and satire of the comedy has always involved risks. This fact became most evident when Chappelle left his show—and a multi-million-dollar contract—after concerns that people weren't laughing at how his caricatures sent up social stereotypes but at the stereotypes themselves. After a long hiatus, Chappelle returned to stand-up, releasing five comedy specials for Netflix in a mind-boggling two-year span. (We are not aware of anybody who has produced this level of comedy in such a short period before.) But these specials have also taken risks. Despite praise from some, many have taken issue with Chappelle's seemingly retrograde views on gender and transgender issues, claiming the comedian has resorted to punching down for cheap laughs among the barstool sports crowd.

We talk about the idea of "punching down" later in this book. Here, we won't attempt to adjudicate the ethics of Chappelle's comedy—whether he crossed too many lines on *Chappelle's Show* or more recently in his Netflix specials. The point is this: The risks are inherent to the way he approaches satire and what he understands the targets of satire to be. The controversies are signals not just of his importance but also of the novelty of his comedy. Chappelle's satire, in the grand American tradition, is couched not in studied or sophisticated terms but in everyday language, wearing the clothes of common sense. The characters, punchlines, and voices in Chappelle's jokes are often deliberately stripped of nuance and subtlety—sometimes including his own onstage persona—in order to send up the self-serious and self-righteous.

But just because someone is self-righteous doesn't mean he or she isn't also correct. Approaching serious and often morally important topics—whether it be crack addiction, interracial relationships, or transphobia—as Chappelle does, with the affected simplicity of a Twain character transported from the Mississippi to post–civil rights black America, means sometimes stepping on the toes of those with legitimate grievances. Mocking the pretensions of the self-assured often means the right-minded are mocked along with the powerful, even if the former have God on their side.

The righteous are as likely to be felled by the satirical sword as those on the wrong side of history. Satirists always have a perspective and a moral angle, but in a way that differs from the activist or the advocate: they privilege the punchline over the policy, the comedy over collective action. This means that comics will always attract their share of critics. But satire's tendency to avoid political pronouncement doesn't make it nihilistic. Our natural inclination toward satirizing politics doesn't mean we naturally retreat from politics. Quite the contrary! In fact, satire's emphasis on producing laughter over lasting change allows it to accomplish things that other forms of political speech and political action cannot.

Satire and jokes *can* serve a political purpose even when they're not preaching a cause. This is because joke telling and chop busting have other features that are socially important. Calling out those in power and pointing out the ridiculous doesn't challenge only the powerful and ridiculous. Comedy works not just "vertically" but also "horizontally": it challenges the audience to think and interact differently as citizens in ways that are congenial to political life.

Sammy Basu points out a number of ways that humor is politically useful.[12] On the one hand, living in a culture where comedy is treasured and encouraged alters the way we think in important, useful ways. Humor "dilates the mind"—it allows us to be playful with ideas that we normally would feel the need to treat seriously. Chappelle's "Reparations" sketch or Pryor's recounting of his own experiences with drugs are now classic examples. A great recent example of this concept is comedian Jeremy McLellan discussing the gender pay gap and the statistic that says that women make seventy-seven cents for every dollar that a man makes. In his routine, McLellan jokes that he thinks the pay gap is justified: "I think men should make more than women . . . because we provide for women. We end up sharing all that extra money with our wives and daughters to take care of them." If you listen to this on YouTube,[13] you can hear audience members getting upset by this assertion. But McLellan, with a puckish grin, continues, "Which can get really expensive, because I don't know if you know this, they only make seventy-seven cents for every dollar a man makes. So, if anything, we should be getting a raise!" It's a great bit, but what's so effective about it is that it doesn't try to stake out a position or really claim anything particularly substantive at all. Instead, it takes a political idea and takes it seriously by playing with it. Instead of telling you what he thinks or what you ought to think, McLellan invites the audience to reflect on what *they* think, by momentarily making it the object of fun and silliness, instead of righteous seriousness.

This ability for playfulness is important in politics because it allows us to think about things in ways we normally wouldn't allow ourselves to try. Often politics can overly regiment our opinions and thoughts. We frequently take on the views and assumptions of "our team" without thinking.[14] Humor has the unique ability to disrupt this tendency by giving us license to let our guard down and laugh at things, without forgetting that they are important. As a consequence, we become more receptive to ideas and perspectives than we normally are. Even better, humor can get us to recognize how narrow minded we often are. Comedy doesn't just get us to look at things differently; it also invites us to think about how we think about things. A wise-cracking comedian, making light of things we take seriously, forces us to reflect on ourselves and how we act and think when politically engaged.

This idea leads to a second way that Basu thinks humor is helpful, which is that it alters our political dispositions. By being playful with the serious and important, comedy pushes us to be a bit more modest in our political disagreements and confrontations with others. If we can reflect on ourselves and our rigid thinking, we are nudged into thinking about our political foes in different ways. Maybe our differences aren't so big! Or "Yes, our differences are that big, but I have been wrong before too." If we approach those with whom we disagree in such a fashion, we are better dispositioned for constructive engagement.

A comedic disposition allows for disagreements to be hashed out and aired without us killing each other. If humor has the cognitive benefit of allowing us to think about things with our guard down, it also allows us to engage others in a similar way. We can argue—and, indeed, argue vehemently—but in a slightly more relaxed, "lubricated" fashion. We can simultaneously say "it's just a joke" while acknowledging that "many a true word is spoken in jest." If war is politics by other means, then having a disposition toward comedy allows us to avoid this deadly and horrible option, the violence that is always just around the corner, by recourse to jokes. Aristotle famously suggested that a good citizen must be able to rule and be ruled in turn. To this statement we might add that a good citizen must be able to bust chops and have their chops busted in turn.

This disposition also allows for a kind of solidarity to form. Many have noticed that the late Supreme Court justice Antonin Scalia was very good friends with his political foes, including especially fellow Supreme Court justices Ruth Bader Ginsburg and Elena Kagan. This situation was aided, surely, by his famous sense of humor, which even those who loathed his politics and jurisprudence had to concede. Stephen Colbert tells the story of his infamous 2006 White House Correspondents' Dinner address, at which a comedian roasts the president and the rest of the assembled Washington luminaries. Colbert famously skewered then president George W. Bush a bit more pointedly than his predecessors, which was greeted with silence and averted glances. But Colbert tells us the one person who was laughing hysterically was Justice Scalia, whom Colbert had actually personally targeted in his roast.[15]

Indeed, presidential roasts can often be harsh. Colbert, admonishing critics of the Bush administration who likened it to the *Titanic*, claimed that the Bush administration "was soaring. It's more like the Hindenburg!" Or think of Michelle Wolf's instant classic joke at the expense of Sarah Huckabee Sanders, White House press secretary: "I actually really like Sarah. I think she's very resourceful. She burns facts, and then she uses the ash to create a perfect smoky eye. Maybe she's born with it; maybe it's lies. It's probably lies."

These jokes show that the ability to share a laugh together doesn't excuse our political opponents their potentially noxious views. Scalia's jokes and guffaws certainly never stopped Ginsburg, Kagan, or Colbert from strongly criticizing and rebuking him for his originalist jurisprudence or his views, say, on abortion or gender. But it does allow us to remember what it is we are disagreeing about—namely, a common project to which we are all committed. In putting aside our disagreements and collectively laughing at something, we acknowledge that, despite our differences, we are still doing something together.

These positive political side effects of humor lead to an interesting question: Does comedy make not just better citizens but also better practices? Some think so, that comedy and satire are uniquely democratic and uniquely conducive to promoting a healthy democracy.

In some sense there is an obvious connection between the two: comedy usually involves dissent and challenge, and dictators don't generally have great senses of humor. Modern democracies, by guaranteeing freedom of speech and the ability to communicate dissent, are more hospitable environments for satire. So, democracy is good for humor. But the question remains: Is humor good for democracy? Do satire and joke telling help us achieve and keep stable democratic government?

Maybe, but maybe not. While comedy can help us be better citizens by encouraging a type of playfulness, it might do this too much! Many think democracy requires a certain type of seriousness. After all, playfulness can cut both ways. While it might allow us to stop taking ourselves so seriously, it might also make us take democratic commitments and civil liberties less seriously. Donald Trump, whatever else you might think about him, can be pretty funny. But many worry that his comedy is harmful because it encourages us to take the dignity of our fellow citizens less seriously, as something that we can joke about.

Still, comedy does have democratic benefits. Democracy isn't just good for comedy. Comedy is good for democracy.

According to the Canadian political theorist Simon Lambek, political humor and satire can play a very particular role in a democracy by addressing a particular problem.[16] Ideally, democracy isn't just about people voting for representatives; it also is about citizens having the freedom, means, and disposition to communicate and debate with one another about political ideas, values, and policies. On this "deliberative" view of democracy, the vitality and legitimacy of our government is measured by the level and quality of debate and deliberation and the degree to which institutions and resources enable citizens to participate in this conversation on equal terms.[17]

This is all well and good in theory. But as anybody knows who has witnessed or participated in political debate, deliberation and communication don't always have this sort of effect. Sometimes deliberation gets people to dig their heels in, leading to polarization. Sometimes "debate" can lead to people believing untrue and immoral things. The problem is that sometimes the smartest person in the room is not the most eloquent, and sometimes people committed to misleading others are the most rhetorically compelling in the crowd. Deliberation can be undemocratic when it is not checked and when it allows people to be swayed by the worse argument.

This is where satire and comedy become important, because they can be a useful corrective, pushing deliberation back toward its democratic potential. Humor, as we've seen above, can be uniquely disruptive. Jokes have the special ability to take the conventional wisdom and show us why the convention is silly and perhaps unwise. Why does humor have this special ability to disrupt things in this way? Lambek's answer is simple but ingenious: jokes can do this better than other forms of communication precisely because they're funny.

Rethinking status quos and questioning our basic social beliefs is uncomfortable and not something we are prone to do. What makes humor and satire so important is that they do these things while making us laugh in the process. This keeps us from looking away. The political genius of Dave Chappelle, Jon Stewart, Richard Pryor, George Carlin, or Ali Wong isn't just that their humor involves astute sociopolitical observation or piercing critical insight (though it does). It's also that they are good enough joke tellers that we stick around to listen to the political point they are making. Without the jokes, the political point is for naught. Or, as Chris Rock once put it eloquently, "Whatever gimmick you have, Henny Youngman has to have something to do with it."[18]

Satire serves a democratic purpose best when it is not trying to offer an argument exactly. This idea might seem counterintuitive, but think about it: What could be *less* democratic than one person stating an opinion and a crowd of people passively listening? Satire is at its most democratic when it doesn't give an answer but screws things up enough so that the audience can better see the problem. The comedian won't solve the problem for you—after all, in a democracy we shouldn't want others to solve things for us anyway. Instead, satire invites the audience to think through it on their own. What could be more democratic than that?

Now, Lambek doesn't think all comedy is democratic. When comedy makes us laugh in such a way that it reinforces oppressive patterns or group prejudices, it hinders democracy. In such instances, the laughter that potentially dilates our minds for healthy political engagement turns into a numbing agent, leading us to passively accept prejudices and practices we ought to be questioning.

Still, the basic point is that comedy plays a special role in a democracy. Humor and mockery step in where rational argument stumbles. As we all know, reason is not always the language of life or politics, and trying to apply reason where reason doesn't exist doesn't work. Often times, we need to address life from a skewed satirical point of view. Frederick Douglass famously said that when it came to abolishing slavery in the United States, "scorching irony, not convincing argument, is needed."[19] Why? Because one *can't* reason with someone engaged in something so heinously unreasonable!

Satire is not just another form of political argumentation; it is political argument's necessary complement, which gives vital force and substance to our ongoing social deliberations. We are satirical animals not because we prefer comedy to compassion, jokes to justice, or parody to politics. Satire is a crucial part of the human condition precisely because we *do* care about the social world in which we live.

CHAPTER 4

The Fairer and Funnier Sex

"Comedy is a blood sport. It flays the truth and spurts twisted logic. In America, people become comics because we don't have bullfighting."

—ELAYNE BOOSLER

Since World War II, the state, the staging, and the status of both stand-up and performance comedy (radio, movies, TV sitcoms) have been radically altered. Before the war and well into the early 1970s, comedy was made up of mostly men, dressed up in tailored suits or tuxedos, rattling off a long list of one-liners and shaggy-dog stories. There were, however, two interesting exceptions to this rule.

Milton Berle was the star of *The Texaco Star Theatre* TV show (1948–1956) and regularly opened the show doing a routine dressed as a woman. The other was Flip Wilson of the *Flip Wilson Show* (1970–1974), who regularly played the character Geraldine Jones, a sassy modern woman whose boyfriend's name was Killer.

The number of female comedians working on stage, screen, TV, and radio or doing stand-up was by no means miniscule, but they nonetheless numbered much fewer than their male counterparts. Some claim that the discrepancy between male and female comic performances was in excess of four to one.[1] There are a number of reasons behind the dearth of women in comedy: simple custom and tradition, comedy/buffoonery being considered unladylike, and a rather malicious form of male chauvinism that adamantly maintained that women, by nature, were not very funny. Women fought hard to win a foothold in comedy. And that struggle is nicely captured in Amazon Prime's hit series *The Marvelous Mrs. Maisel*.

Johnny Carson (1925–2005) was once the king of late-night TV talk shows and the "maker or breaker" of comedic careers. To be invited to do five minutes on *The Tonight Show Starring Johnny Carson* was to be summoned to the cathedral of comedy. If Pope Johnny laughed and liked you, a successful career in show business could almost be guaranteed. A "thumbs-down," however, meant, at best, a lifetime of three shows a night for bad money at "Sal's Hideaway," "Mannie's Man Cave," or "Al's Strip Joint." Although Carson helped launch the career of a number of female comics, women were the exception and not the rule on his show.

In a 1979 interview for *Rolling Stone*, Carson said that comedy is a pretty rough and tough business, adding, "I think it's much tougher on women." Consequently, "you don't see many of them around. And the ones that try . . . are a little too aggressive for my taste. I'll take it from a guy, but from a woman, sometimes it just doesn't fit too well." Ironically, the one female Carson regularly had on his show was Joan Rivers. But, perhaps because Rivers was so busy telling self-deprecating jokes and satirizing how women and wives go about their lives, Carson was not threatened or offended by her.[2] Rivers's first appearance on *The Tonight Show* was in 1965, and Carson liked her so much that in 1983 he "crowned" her as his first "permanent guest host." Their mutual admiration society lasted until Rivers signed to do her own late-night show on Fox in 1986 and neglected to inform Carson about her signing. Carson felt betrayed and banned Rivers from his show. The ban was enforced long after Carson's retirement and death. It wasn't until Jimmy Fallon took over *The Tonight Show* in 2014 that she returned to the show that started her career.

Another male mogul of contemporary comedy who found the "fairer sex" fair but not funny was Jerry Lewis. While most millennials have, at best, a passing awareness of Jerry Lewis, many baby boomers think of him as a "clownish, comedic god." The French thought of him as the "Great Jerry," America's major contribution to comedy and films, and "one of the greatest performers and comic minds of the 20th century."[3]

At the US Comedy Arts Festival in Aspen, Colorado, in 1998, during a Q&A conducted by fellow comedian Martin Short, Lewis was asked whether he liked Lucille Ball. His response: "I don't like any female comedians. A woman doing comedy doesn't offend me but sets me back a bit. I, as a viewer, have trouble with it. I think of her as a producing machine that brings babies in the world."[4]

According to entertainment columnist Eliana Dockerman, the question "Are women funny in today's world of comedy?" is a ridiculous query. Just look at the long litany of female comedians who have stepped into the spotlight since the 1970s.[5] To name a few: Issa Ray, Tracee Ellis Ross, Tina Fey, Amy Poehler, Julia Louis-Dreyfus, Maya Rudolph, Chelsea Handler, Liza Schlesinger, Amy Schumer, Ali Wong, Tig Notaro, Hannah Gadsby, Ellen DeGeneres, Michelle Wolf, Whitney Cummings, Wanda Sykes, Kathy Griffin, Tiffany Haddish, Paula Poundstone, Janeane Garofalo, Samantha Bee, Mindy Kaling, Aisha Tyler, Carmen Esposito, Natasha Leggero, Ali Wentworth, and Gina Rodriguez.

The female stand-up boom of the 1960s and 1970s was a crucial development in comedy. But it was not a "one-theme-fits-all" experience. Different women brought different points of view to the party. Each comic brought different sensibilities to her act. Some told "anti-women" jokes. Some told "stupid husband" jokes. Some told "insult jokes"—about everyone and everything.

Some told "sex jokes" ranging in severity from innocent, naughty double entendres to nasty, dominatrix vignettes. Some told jokes making fun of stay-at-home moms, house cleaning, feminism, lesbians, and librarians; there were some really naughty vegetarian howlers! Some joked about self-abuse. Others talked about misogyny. Some told jokes about being gay or being gray. Unfortunately, it can be argued that too many of these jokes were self-deprecating, abusive, and antiwomen. Too often they reinforced the "unsaid" stereotype of women as irrational, ditzy, and somewhat childish. But perhaps part of their humor, part of their charm, part of their general accept-ability was that these jokes about women were now being told *by* women. Perhaps part of the pleasure was that you now had women making you laugh about the vicis-situdes of daily life with the same sense of innocence and playfulness that Henny Youngman practiced throughout his career, sometimes with a good dose of sexist shtick. For example: "Last week a thief stole all my wife's credit cards. But I haven't reported it to the police because the thief is spending a lot less than my wife would have!" Or this one: "Secret to a happy marriage? Simple, it is din-ner and dancing two nights a week. I go on Tuesdays. She goes on Thursdays!"

It can be argued that the reigning queen of com-edy during those days was Phyllis Diller. Diller was an unexpected late bloomer. She was a forty-one-year-old housewife from California who just wanted to be funny and get away from her six kids and her ne'er-do-well husband.

She made her professional debut at San Francisco's Purple Onion in 1955 and got her national break in 1958 on *The Jack Paar Show*. She quickly became a pop-cultural icon on TV and in clubs. She played the role of the crazed housewife with wild, electrified hair, wearing miniskirts and flamboyant boas. Her delivery was rapid-fire and nonstop. In a one-hour set, she told one one-liner after another about her husband, the kids, her body, her clothes, and the failures and fallacies of domestic life.

I've been asked to say a few words about my husband, Fang. OK, how about "short" and "cheap"!

Fang is so inept—he couldn't sell Windex to a peeping Tom!

Sexually, nothing much is happening in my marriage. I nicknamed our waterbed Lake Placid!

I spent hours in the beauty shop last week—and that was just for an estimate!

I once had a peek-a-boo blouse. People would peek, and then they would boo!

Diller's popularity was based on her ability to make fun of herself and please a crowd. She was a consummate performer in the tradition of vaudeville, the borscht belt, and the night club circuit. She knew her job, and she did it well. Her objective was to entertain, to titillate, and to get a laugh. She was in show business, and she told jokes intended to please, to provide a smile. None of her routines were sociologically or politically profound or prophetic. She wasn't out to change the world. She was trying to earn a living and have a few laughs along the way.

For a long time, it was standard practice for women comedians to focus their routines on their flaws and failures as females. And then, in the late 1970s and the 1980s, the range of options and the general repertoire of female comics began to change. Women were increasingly telling jokes with a bite, a message, not just a punchline, speaking truth through humor in order to detoxify and disarm various social stereotypes. And a leading agent of change in this comedic metamorphosis was the ever-flamboyant Joan Rivers.

Joan Rivers, however, did not begin her career as an antiestablishment provocateur and satirical commentator on gender issues, celebrities in the news, and the fashion industry. Like her role model Lenny Bruce and her contemporary George Carlin, Rivers started her career telling jokes, any kind of jokes, and trying to get a laugh. Like so many of her contemporary female comics, she told self-deprecating jokes, mother jokes, and men jokes. (Husband jokes only became part of the act after she married in her mid-thirties.)

> My parents hated me. My present for my first birthday was luggage.

> For bath toys, my parents gave me a toaster and a radio.

> Early in my career, I had a terrible job. I was a topless dancer—in a gay bar.

> It wasn't easy when I started. All I could give my agent was 10% of the tomatoes they threw at me.

> As I approached 30, and I was still single, my mother got desperate. She put a sign up on the lawn . . . "Last girl before the Thru-way."

According to Rivers, she began to be a better comedian during her short stint at Chicago's now famous Second City. She said that Second City taught her how to deliver jokes and not just repeat them. She learned how to really *sell* a joke, enabling her to do a different kind of comedy.[6] She began to discover a personal point of view. She was a woman stand-up in a man's world. She realized that she had something special to say, and she began to say it. Her jokes were no longer simply self-deprecating. Yes, she talked about being a woman. Yes, she talked about dating, men, marriage, kids, fashion, aging—the usual topics of life—but now she had an angle to go along with her edge.

The Joan Rivers we now recognize and remember came to be on February 17, 1965, when by good fate she was shoehorned into the last ten-minute slot of *The Tonight Show*. She so charmed Johnny that night with her smart, satirical take on life that he said to her on air, "God, you're funny. You're going to be a star."[7] Building on her "few minutes of fame," Rivers made herself into a comic critic of contemporary life. "Politics" (in the formal, institutional sense of the word) she only occasionally flirted with. But women's lives, women's fashion, marriage, children, celebrities, friends, and all things connected to show business and the public forum were fodder and fertilizer for her caustic comic wit. Roseanne Barr once said, "Comics are angry people with something to say!"[8] Joan Rivers always had something to say: "A man can sleep around, no questions asked. But if a woman makes 19 or 20 mistakes, she's a tramp."

Rivers's brand of satire was a radical departure from that of many of the men who came before her. Take Mort Sahl's style onstage as an example. Sahl was a mild, soothing Mr. Rogers in comparison to Rivers with her jagged barbs. Although she was always glamorously dressed onstage, Rivers was boisterous, bawdy, and over the top in her delivery. She assaulted the audience with her voice, her gestures, and her dynamism. Her performance was not a careful, quiet deconstruction of an interesting or curious cultural phenomenon. Her style was to attack and overwhelm both the topic and her audience with her raw energy and physicality. Hers was a Genghis Khan, full-frontal, kick-in-the-genitalia, ad hominem assault. And when she went over the top and the audience gasped, she'd stop, glare at them, and then yell, "Can we talk? Grow up! These are just jokes."

For Rivers, jokes were a way of dealing with the serious topics, silly topics, deep topics, and unavoidable topics of life without being defeated or scared to death by them. For Rivers, laughter and joke telling were ways of dealing with the good, the bad, and the ugly. As she said, over and over again, "If you can laugh at it, you can live with it."[9]

Perhaps the most delicious part of Rivers's satirical wit was her ability to make fun of the lifestyle that she herself chose to live. In 2009, she published a book, the title of which she claimed spoke to the core of her philosophical and comedic beliefs concerning women and happiness: *Men Are Stupid . . . and They Like Big Boobs*.[10] The main points of the text in some sense represent the sum total of her personal and comedic beliefs regarding society's perspective on women:

> Looks matter! Don't bother to cook. Don't bother to clean. No man will ever make love to a woman because she waxed the linoleum—"My God, the floor's immaculate. Lie down, you hot bitch!"

> Forget inner-beauty. If a man wants inner-beauty, he'll take x-rays.

Rivers argues that being sexy means taking care of yourself, by whatever means necessary. "God may have created my nose," said Rivers, "but he also created the plastic surgeon to fix it."[11] Although Rivers never admitted to the exact number of surgeries she underwent (published guestimates ranged from 30 to 348 to 739), one can confidently say she had multiple procedures. In her uniquely outrageous (yet charming) way, Joan Rivers's brand of comedy gave life to a line from Picasso: "Art is a lie that makes us realize the truth."

Joan Rivers served as a role model for a generation of up-and-coming female comedians, one of them being Sarah Silverman. There were, of course, some real differences between the two. To begin with, as one fashionista pointed out, Silverman is "usually dressed like a 14-year old boy—T-shirt, jeans, and well-worn Adidas."[12] She usually "dresses as if she's always ready for a touch-football game."[13] One of her business managers once told her that she "spent the least amount of money on clothes of any client I've ever had, male or female."[14] Silverman has said that she has a fear of clothing and that she "feels like a transvestite when I'm all dressed up."[15] Also different from Rivers, who stormed onto the stage with the stride of a queen and the vocal chops of a circus ringmaster, Silverman moves on to the stage in a more modest fashion and delivers her insights and zingers in a calm and well-modulated voice.

As far as we can determine from our research, Sarah Silverman has never told any kind of joke resembling "A priest, a rabbi, and a minister walk into a bar . . ." or "Did you hear the one about . . . ?" According to NPR's cultural guru Terry Gross, Silverman doesn't tell jokes. Rather, she makes fearless "social commentary" that happens to be funny, making her perhaps more like her contemporary Chris Rock than Joan Rivers.[16] Silverman is ironic, iconoclastic, illogical, irritating, irreverent, and, at times, a demented commentator on the world around her. She is "someone who says things she doesn't mean and (through more-or-less subtle contextual winks) expects us to intuit her understated, smaller message underneath it all."[17] According to Sam Anderson of *Slate*, Silverman's best jokes (and often her most vulgar and naughty) are thought experiments and twists on the internal logic of political correctness in regard to social traditions, myths, and long-held beliefs.[18] And her wit knows no boundaries. She prides herself on being an equal-opportunity offender.

The Holocaust would never have happened if Black people lived in Germany in the 1930s and 40s . . . well, it wouldn't have happened to Jews.

I was raped by a doctor. Which is, as you know, bittersweet for a Jewish girl!

I wanted to get an abortion, but my boyfriend and I were having trouble conceiving.

My sister was with two men in one night. She could hardly walk after that.
   Can you imagine? Two whole dinners?

What is it about Christmas that you think that Jews hate? Do you think we hate the giant spike in retail? Is it the royalty checks on every Christmas song?

Once I was summoned to jury duty, but I really didn't want to serve. A friend advised me to avoid serving by writing a racial slur on the selection form.

Something inappropriate like, "I hate Chinks." But,
I decided that was too racist, so I wrote—"I love
Chinks, who doesn't?"

Silverman delivers these jokes, and many more of the same, with a straight face and just the slightest gleam in her eye. She believes that often you can't change people's minds with facts and logic. Instead, sometimes our best bet is to try to change perceptions by prompting people to respond to the world around them in surprising ways. For Silverman, comedy doesn't always succeed in changing minds. But at least it can offer alternative points of view and another way of looking at things. And the most immediate way to do that is through searing satire and laughter.

Perhaps the most telling comedic difference between Rivers and Silverman is that for Rivers, political jokes were a "one-off." That is, if there was a massive story in the news or political gaff that was "low-hanging fruit," Rivers went for it and then returned to her comfort zone: celebrities, fashion, show business, and an unending series of straightforward sexual jokes and double entendres. By contrast, Silverman's commentary is always political in nature. When she talks about sex, friendship, families, work, or play, she's talking about politics—that is, "the power plays and power struggles and strategies that individuals negotiate and employ when dealing with others." For example: "I [Silverman] love being in a relationship, working together to achieve a common goal. His orgasm!"

Like Joan Rivers, Margaret Cho is all about being unapologetic in pushing the limits and stretching the boundaries of her comedic persona. Like Sarah Silverman, Cho believes that the guise of comedy gives her permission and freedom to explore and examine any topic or subject matter that attracts her attention. All three of these women are equally convinced that although comedy is not always a corrective or a cure, it can be the catalyst for change. In making fun of something, in satirically highlighting a situation, comedy is often (but not always) suggesting, "Look, laugh, and think! Sometimes if we make fun of it, we can transcend it!"[19]

Cho's life as a contrarian and a comic started long before she walked onstage and did her first stand-up routine. She was born Margaret Moran Cho on December 5, 1968, in San Francisco. The name "Moran" in Korean means peony flower. Her classmates, of course, pronounced it "moron." Hence, she engendered laughter long before she even knew what being funny meant!

Growing up in the Haight-Ashbury district of San Francisco, the epicenter of gay and hippy counterculture in the 1970s, was perfect fodder for a budding comic mind. And then there were Cho's family dynamics to deal with, along with her growing sexual curiosity and interests. To her friends and classmates, although she was born in America, she never felt like a "real" American girl. (Read "real" as "white.") And at home, her parents constantly harangued her for not being a "good Korean girl." She didn't play the violin. She wasn't a good student. And she didn't want to be a doctor. Sexually, Cho admits that as far back as she can remember, she was "open and interested" in all forms of sexual encounters and activity. She has alternatively defined herself as a "fag hag," bisexual, gay, straight, married (Al Ridenour, 2003–2015), omnivorous, and/or just a plain old-fashioned slut: "I'm just slutty. So, where's my parade? What about slut pride?"

Because of all of this, Cho claims that she was ineluctably drawn to comedy. She saw the world from the perspective of always being different, always being an outsider. She felt she had a date, a calling, to "rumble with stupidity, ignorance, and prejudice."[20] Being an outsider sensitized her to the issues of other outsiders and all issues that impact negatively on those who cannot defend themselves. Her comedy tries to shed light on political, racial, and ethnic prejudices and stereotypes—from homophobia to society's obsession with "beauty" to abortion, addiction and alcoholism, gay and lesbian rights, civil rights, obesity, and the abuses of the American penal system. Nothing is above or beyond her reproach and criticism.

Cho was, and is, consciously bipolar in her approach to comedy as an art form and a tool for communication. She truly believes that as an art form, comedy is a "gift from the gods" that has the transcendental power to allow us to, at least momentarily, forget our problems, add hilarity to the human condition, and overcome our fears of the known and unknown. Humor allows us the space to "recognize that being different is the norm" and that all human experience is varied. Humor has the ability to transcend the simply given facts of the world. Humor allows us to transcend boundaries imposed by race, ethnicity, sexual preference, and ideological, religious, political, and aesthetic differences.[21] Humor is a celebration of life. It allows us to laugh at and with life.[22] Humor allows us to overcome fear, hate, our deepest bigotry with regard to others, and our own episodes of self-loathing. When we collectively laugh at the same things, we realize that we have a lot more in common than we thought.[23]

Although Cho's philosophical explanations of the range and powers of comedy and humor are nuanced and cerebral, her stage performance is anything but delicate or subtle. Onstage, she is an energized, raging, ribald, raunchy, lecherous, and licentious "siren skewer" of social hypocrisy and political self-centeredness. She is bombastically loud and "in-your-face" confrontational with her audience, deploying a vocabulary that might make Carlin blush.

She comes out swinging—"Haven't we heard enough from these ancient white guys?"[24]—questioning, among other things, how well the whole "blessed are the meek" idea is working out for us.[25] By her own admission, Cho can be an "assertive, unapologetic, demanding bitch." And she owns it. She embraces it as a compliment rather than a criticism. It's who she is. She believes it's what a comic is supposed to do: talk about stuff nobody really feels comfortable talking about.

Cho believes that in order to deal with entrenched stupidity, ignorance, prejudice, laziness, hatred, and greed, you have to go toe-to-toe with it.[26] You have to "utter—make that scream—the untenable."[27] You have to get their attention, take risks, and make them listen. Educate, but be funny! Even though her critics haven't always agreed with her, comedy for Cho should be a natural blend of personal involvement or awareness, social issues and activism, and good dick jokes.[28]

I slept with this woman, and afterwards I got to thinking: Am I gay? Am I straight? Then I realized: No, I'm just slutty.

Any society that tries to prevent a gay man from opening a bridal registry at a major department store is a fascist state!

I love my gay male friends! When I was a little girl, I always used to wish that I would be constantly surrounded by gorgeous guys with big dicks, and I am! But I should have been more specific.

I don't know why Republicans hate gay marriage so. My experience is that they certainly don't hate gay prostitutes!

All three of these women—Joan Rivers, Sarah Silverman, and Margaret Cho—have spent their careers clinically observing and investigating the social and political mores of their lives and times. But very importantly, they have been part of the scene they are reporting on. They have lived it. They have experienced it directly. They are "wise fools" examining and offering analysis and criticism of the world around them. But they don't do this as dispassionate third parties, observing the ridiculousness of the world with a scholar's remove. The political insights of their satire come precisely from the very personal stakes such things have for them.

Feminists in the 1960s popularized the slogan "The personal is political." The idea was to galvanize political action and awareness through the recognition that one's "personal" life was affected by social distributions of power and resources—the structure of one's family life, the patterns of one's intimate relationships, and so on are not just private choices that people make but also reflections of how society constrains and affects our choices. The same thing is true of jokes: a bit about personal experiences is often also a comment on the social facts that make that experience so common to so many. Male critics often miss this point about female comics. Amy Schumer has pointed out that because she talks about sex in her act, she's labeled a sex comic. As she notes, though, this is a double standard: "I think it's because I'm a girl. I feel like a guy could come out here and pull his dick out and people would say 'Oh, he's a thinker.'"[29]

When a man tells a sex joke, he's being edgy. When a woman does it, it's dirty. Though that's the common prejudice, we think the opposite is actually true. What would just be a sex joke in the hands of Rodney Dangerfield or Kevin Smith becomes a political joke in the hands of someone like Silverman or Cho. In their hands, the sex joke also becomes a satirical take on the power dynamics and social expectations that inform relationships between men and women and a criticism of how women are socialized to engage with the world.

CHAPTER 5

Why Are Jews So Funny?

"Whoever has cried enough, laughs!"

—HEINRICH MANN

In the 1960s, the Jewish population in America was less than 3 percent, but, according to *Time* magazine, nearly 80 percent of the top-performing comedians were Jewish. As one pundit put it, "Comedy in America was a Jewish cottage industry!"[1] In contrast to performers like Jackie Mason, Myron Cohen, Henny Youngman, Joan Rivers, and Lenny Bruce, who openly identified with and poked fun at their Jewish heritage, most successful comedians anglicized their names and crafted a comic persona and a repertoire of jokes that appealed to a general audience—for example, Jack Benny (Benjamin Kubelsky), George Burns (Nathan Bienhaum), Jerry Lewis (Jerome Levitch), Rodney Dangerfield (Jacob Cohen), and Red Buttons (Aaron Chwatt). Today's comedy scene is no longer as completely dominated by Jewish performers. But no-nonsense Jewish names are still major players in the world of show business: Jerry Seinfeld, Paul Reiser,

David Steinburg, Larry David, Marc Maron, Sacha Baron Cohen, Amy Schumer, Sarah Silverman, Judd Apatow, Adam Sandler, Seth Rogan, Fran Drescher, and Vanessa Bayer.

Given these names and numbers, the trick question is "Are Jews predisposed to comedy?" Answer: Genetically predisposed or programmed for comedy and shtick, no, we don't think so. Claiming that Jews or any other ethnic or racial group possess a specific gene or cluster of comedic genes is, at best, dubious and cannot be empirically substantiated. But to the question "Are Jews historically and culturally predisposed to comedy?" the answer is an emphatic yes! Given the title and thesis of this book, we think that one other question begs to be answered: "Are Jewish comics predisposed to satire?" After years of research on this topic, we've come up with a series of very Jewish responses: "Yes and no!" "Sometimes!" "It happens!" "Every once in a while!" "Not so much!" "Maybe?" And last, but not least, "Depends on the comic and the joke!" This, we think, is closest to the mark. Overall, Jewish jokes tend to be sarcastic, cynical, complaining, kvetching in nature. (Think Richard Lewis!) Jewish comics tell a lot of "woe-is-me" type jokes. Woody Allen is a mixture of Nietzschean melancholy, Freudian angst, and Humean skepticism. Mel Brooks, by contrast, is the clever clown who uses over-the-top parody and burlesque imitation to deliver his comic point of view. But whether the type of humor is strictly satirical or "pie-in-the-face" slapstick, much, if not all, Jewish humor is an attempt to deal with the banalities, mysteries, and horrors of life.

Jeremy Dauber, in his recent book *Jewish Comedy: A Serious History*, argues that all of Jewish humor is based on seven social-cultural commonalities:

1. Jewish comedy is a response to persecution and anti-Semitism.

2. Jewish comedy is a satirical gaze at Jewish social and communal norms.

3. Jewish comedy is bookish, witty, intellectual allusive play.

4. Jewish comedy is vulgar, raunchy, and body obsessed.

5. Jewish comedy is mordant, ironic, and metaphysically oriented.

6. Jewish comedy is focused on the folksy, everyday, quotidian Jew.

7. Jewish comedy is about the blurred and ambiguous nature of Jewishness itself.[2]

We could not agree more, at least in regard to the first proposition. However, items 2–7 are not unique or exclusive to the Jewish experience. They are, in fact, cultural touchstones or phenomena that transcend any claim of exclusivity or ethnic originality and are the source or stimulus for jokes in many other cultures. A cursory check into the "comic archives" will quickly result in the discovery of a variety of non-Jewish-based jokes that fit into these categories.

2: A SATIRICAL GAZE AT SOCIAL COMMUNAL NORMS

Germans are flummoxed by humor, the Swiss have no concept of fun, the Spanish think there is nothing at all ridiculous about eating dinner at midnight, and the Italians should never, ever have been let in on the invention of the motorcar.

—Bill Bryson

An Indian father's admonition to his teenage son: "No parties! No fooling around! No girls! No dating! Fun doesn't start until medical school!"

—Hasan Minhaj

3: BOOKISH, WITTY, AND INTELLECTUAL

A psychiatrist was at his office late one night when he heard a very faint tapping at his door. When he opened it, he found a rather large moth hovering in front of him. Suddenly, the moth began to speak and complain about the quality of his life and how unhappy he was. According to the moth, he was feeling depressed and suicidal and he asked the psychiatrist whether he would take him on as a client. "Yes, of course," said the psychiatrist, "but why me? Why now?" The moth stared at him quizzically and said, "Because your light was on!"

—A version of Norm Macdonald's "Moth and the Podiatrist" joke.

4: Vulgar, Raunchy, and Body Obsessed

A guy walks into an Irish pub and sees a sign that says:

Cheese Sandwiches—$4.00

Hand Jobs—$10.00

He walks up to the waitress and says, "Excuse me, are you the one who gives the hand jobs?"

"Yes, I am!" she says smilingly.

"Well, please go wash your hands, because I would like a cheese sandwich!"

A fellow got arrested last Saturday. He was standing out in his backyard with just his pajama tops on. His neighbor asked him, "What'cha doing out in the backyard with just your pajama tops on?"

He says, "Last week, I went to the drugstore and I didn't have a scarf on, so I got a stiff neck. This is my wife's idea."

—Redd Foxx

5: Mordant, Ironic, and Metaphysical

In 1900, Oscar Wilde was dying of meningitis in a run-down, horribly decorated Parisian hotel. Deeply depressed by his surroundings and in his failing health, Wilde reportedly quipped to a friend, "My wallpaper and I are fighting a duel to the death. One or the other of us has to go."

6: Folksy, Everyday, Quotidian

The only way I could have friends eat at my house was to brief them before they came over: ". . . Listen to me and listen good. When you're done with the meal, if you want a little more, it's going to get very tricky. Don't tell my mother you want a little more, because then she'll serve you a whole new meal. . . . You want a little? Tell her you want no more. You want a lot more? Tell her you want a little. You really don't want any more? You have to shoot her."

—Ray Romano

Ole was on his first date with Lena, and he took her to the New Ulm. In the restaurant Ole said, "Hey, Lena, would you like a cocktail before dinner?"

"Oh, no, Ole," said Lena. "What would I tell my Sunday School class?"

After dinner, he said, "Hey would you like a cigarette?"

"Oh, no, Ole," said Lena. "What would I tell my Sunday School class?"

Ole was driving Lena home when they passed the Romeo Motel. He said, "Hey, Lena, how would you like to stop at that motel with me?"

"Yah, Ole, dot would be nice," said Lena.

Ole asked, "But vat are you going to tell your Sunday School class?"

"The same ting I always tell them. You don't have to smoke and drink to have a good time!"

—A Wisconsin/Minnesota Scandinavian farmer joke

7: Blurred and Ambiguous Cultural Identity

If you go to family reunions to pick up girls, guess what? You just might be a redneck!

—Jeff Foxworthy

A Greek and an Italian are debating who has the superior culture. The Greek says, "We have the Parthenon." The Italian says, "We have the Colosseum." The Greek says, "We had great mathematicians and philosophers." The Italian says, "We created a world empire and established Pax Romana." And so on and so on, for hours, until the Greek lights up and says, "We invented sex!"

The Italian nods slowly, thinks, and replies, "That is true—but it was Italians who introduced it to women!"

I'm from Finland, and I've been working for a long time trying to look, sound, and be as American as possible. I'm thinking of taking an easy way out: Get fat, stop voting, and invade a small country in the Middle East!

—Lisa Mannerkoski

Putting aside Dauber's first rubric for a moment, we would argue that any attempt to define and catalog a list of jokes and subjects exclusive to the Jewish experience and only told by Jews is doomed to failure. The subject matter and comic punchlines of most (but not all) Jewish shtick and goyim bits are more often than not gleaned from experiences, events, and common existential challenges that are universal to the human condition. Topics such as religion, God, death, illness, marriage and sex (clearly two separate topics), husbands, wives, lovers, friends, adversaries, enemies, in-laws, former in-laws, mothers, stepmothers, neighbors, work, money, jobs, careers, and politics are not exclusive to one ethnic or religious group or moment in time.

There are, of course, cultural differences in the setup and delivery of these "universal joke topics." Accents, emphasis, timing, and body language coat these general topics with a certain parochial tone and color. But we want to argue that a well-constructed joke about marriage, for example, stripped of its parochial particulars makes sense and is funny to a general audience. For example:

A wife [fill in the ethnic group or religious affiliation of your choice] comes home suddenly in the middle of the day and runs into the house. She slams the door and shouts at the top of her lungs to her husband, "Honey, pack your bags. I just won the super lottery!" The husband [ditto, in his regard] says, "Oh my God! That's great! What should I pack, beach stuff or mountain stuff?" "Doesn't matter," the wife screams. "Just get out!"

However, we would argue that there are four joke topics that, although universal in nature, when told by a Jewish comic, often contain a different subtext and poignancy that is part and parcel of American Jewish cultural experience: mothers, wives, daughters, and money.

We note that these sorts of jokes draw on themes that are also familiar anti-Semitic tropes and archetypes: the JAP (Jewish American Princess); the neurotic, overbearing Jewish woman; the penny-pinching cheapskate; and so forth. It is perhaps not surprising, then, that many famous Jewish comedians, satirists, and artists (Woody Allen, Jon Stewart, Philip Roth, Sarah Silverman, etc.) often find so many critics among their fellow tribesmen who affix to them the label of that other great anti-Semitic archetype: the self-hating Jew. We leave for others to debate whether the use of these jokes is in fact morally problematic in some way or what sociological reasons there might be for the overlap between the jokes that Jews make and enjoy and the centuries-old themes of Judeophobia.

We also note that these topics have little to do with Judaism as a religion. This makes some sense: the Torah, the Mishnah, the Talmud, and other religious teachings tend to be a bit more solemn than jocular. Indeed, John Morreal, a philosopher of religion and humor, has maintained that Jewish humor is a secular cultural by-product and not connected to biblical or rabbinic teachings, which tend to have a more tragic worldview.[3] This theory seems accurate enough. However, nothing we say here hinges on this question. On whether Jewish humor is connected to the religious practices of Judaism, we are, if you'll excuse the play on words, agnostic.

According to Sam Hoffman, lifelong Jew and author of *Old Jews Telling Jokes*, Jewish mothers around the world have long served as the head and the heart of the household.[4] They have often been depicted as overprotective, focused, and possessively neurotic regarding the well-being of their families. In America, this legion of driven and determined women meted out tons of laser-focused encouragement and detailed orders to get the job done. And, of course, when that didn't work, there were always the "gifts that keep on giving": guilt, constant nagging, and smothering overprotectiveness. All of this is captured in jokes that acknowledge, applaud, and appreciate the nonstop efforts of Jewish matriarchs while at the same time registering some discomfort and discontent with their nonstop admonishments. For example:

Q: What's a Jewish sweater?

A: A woolen garment worn by a child when their mother gets cold.

Q: The definition of a Jewish genius?

A: An ordinary good boy with a Jewish mother.

Q: At what stage does a Jewish fetus become viable?

A: Only after graduation from medical school.

According to Hoffman, Jewish mothers have created an "art form" out of an admixture of tough love and large portions of smothering adoration. Yet, in spite of all of this, most (but not all) Jewish mother jokes are not vindictive, mean, or denigrating. Rather, they are a backhanded attempt to both critique and celebrate the efforts of Jewish mothers to have their children—especially male children—become the best that they can be.

> Jewish male children are hounded by their mothers to become doctors; and, if they can't become doctors, they can at least become lawyers; and, if they can't become doctors or lawyers and are "not too smart," they can at least become accountants.
>
> —Jackie Mason, former rabbi, comic

For Jewish mothers, behind all this prompting, pushing, and pressure is something much more than simple parochial parental pride. What's at stake is both a personal and a collective agenda, challenge, and goal. It's about achievement, making it, success. And success is much more than getting a job, making a little money, and simple survival. Real success, for a diasporic people, is measured in terms of the ability to control one's destiny. Success means that you are no longer a "stranger in a strange land." Success means that through prodding, effort, energy, and luck, you have arrived. And the success of every Jewish child, it is often felt, adds to the success, stability, and cultural/economic status and well-being of the Jewish community in general. Indeed, by making fun of overbearing Jewish mothers, most comedians are really registering an affection for the milieu that nurtured them and a sort of pride in their accomplishments.

Q: What's the difference between a tailor and a psychiatrist?

A: A generation of hard work and effort!

As two good Jewish boys (well, one Jewish and the other one-eighth Jewish and seven-eighths Italian), we, of course, especially love mother jokes. Here are our big three all-time favorites.

Q: How many Jewish mothers does it take to change a light bulb?

A: (Sigh) Don't bother. I'll sit in the dark. I don't want to be a nuisance or a bother to anybody.

A man called his mother in Florida.

"Mom, how are you?"

"Not too good," said the mother. "I've been very weak."

The son said, "Why are you so weak?"

She said, "Because I haven't eaten in thirty-eight days."

The son said, "That's terrible! Why haven't you eaten in thirty-eight days?!"

The mother answered, "Because I didn't want my mouth to be filled with food if you should finally call!!!"

The year is 2020, and the United States has elected the first woman as well as the first Jewish president, Susan Goldfarb. She calls up her mother a few weeks after Election Day and says, "So, Mom, I assume you'll be coming to my inauguration?"

"I don't think so. It's a ten-hour drive, your father isn't as young as he used to be, and my arthritis is acting up again."

"Don't worry about it, Mom—I'll send Air Force One to pick you up and take you home. A limousine will pick you up at your door."

"I don't know. Everybody will be so fancy-schmancy; what on earth would I wear?"

Susan replies, "I'll make sure you have a wonderful gown custom-made by the best designer in New York."

"Honey," Mom complains, "you know I can't eat those rich foods you and your friends like to eat."

The president-elect responds, "Don't worry, Mom. The entire affair is going to be handled by the best caterer in New York—kosher all the way. Mom, I really want you to come."

So her mother reluctantly agrees, and on January 20, 2021, Susan Goldfarb is sworn in as president of the United States. In the front row sits the new president's mother, who leans over to a senator sitting next to her and says, "You see that woman over there with her hand on the Torah, becoming president of the United States?"

The senator whispers back, "Yes, I do."

Mom says proudly, "Her brother is a doctor!"

By way of an aside, in our research on Jewish mother jokes, the one type of mother joke that was comparatively rare was naughty or sexually explicit mother jokes. Philip Roth's *Portnoy's Complaint* is arguably an example of a giant book-length Jewish mother sex joke, though it is less about the mother's sexuality than the author's own neuroses surrounding sex. The best we were able to find was written and performed by—really, no surprise—Sarah Silverman! But, in her defense, the joke is based on two virtues that are constantly reinforced by all Jewish mothers: (1) always finish what you start, and (2) always clean up after yourself. The joke:

> A couple of nights ago, I was licking jelly off my boyfriend's penis and I thought to myself—"Oh my God, I'm becoming my mother!"

Different from mother jokes, in the Jewish comedic tradition sexual jokes about wives and girlfriends can be just as vulgar, sexist, demeaning, and misogynistic as you will find in Gershon Legman's encyclopedia of lecherous jokes, *Rationale of the Dirty Joke*. However, there exists a subspecies of Jewish jokes about women, wives, and daughters that have a dual meaning. They are both naughty and nice, bragging and complaining, disapproving and boastful, disparaging and celebratory.

Partners complaining about their spouses is, of course, not specific to the Jewish people. Wives of all backgrounds make fun of their husbands' sloppiness or lack of bedroom prowess, and husbands of all backgrounds make the same tired jokes about their wives' and daughters' fiscal excesses and fashion expenditures. But within the Jewish culture, these kinds of jokes, referred to as JAP jokes (the term JAP applies to both wives and daughters), are a double-edged sword. They are part sexist complaints, but they are also braggadocios.

Being able to publicly bemoan the constant excessive spending habits of one's female dependents also suggests that the father/husband can afford to maintain and indulge the women in his life. In complaining, the father/husband in question is simultaneously bragging about his success as a provider, his success in the game of life. In being able to indulge his JAP wife and daughter, he proclaims to the world, "I have arrived, survived, and been assimilated into the larger culture." Like Caesar, he can proudly proclaim, "I came, I conquered, and therefore I can afford to indulge!" This was most famously and best captured in Philip Roth's breakout novella *Goodbye, Columbus*, where the patriarch Mr. Patimkin comments on his son's wedding, "When I got married, we bought knives and forks from the five and ten. This kid needs gold to eat off." But, as the narrator goes on to clarify, "There was no anger [in Mr. Patimkin's voice]; far from it."[5]

The bottom line is that JAP jokes, while hardly without misogynistic undertones, are also often an insecure man's attempts to assure himself and others of male victorious financial virtuosity.

- An American-Jewish patriarch asked that his ashes be scattered in Bloomingdale's so he could be sure his wife and daughter would visit him at least twice a week.

- If a Jewish husband dies in the forest, how long before his wife will go shopping?

- A Jewish wife's perfect house? Seven thousand square feet with no master bedroom, no kitchen, and a private clothes closet the size of a three-car garage.

As Michael Krasny has pointed out, if a Jewish wife or daughter is spoiled or overly indulged, who is the one spoiling that wife or princess daughter? "The credit goes, of course, to the patriarch, the paterfamilias or head of the family—who brings home the not-necessarily kosher bacon!"[6] Those who do not succeed are schlemiels, who constantly kvetch and complain about their fate.

My wife divorced me for religious reasons. She worshipped money, and I didn't have any!

—Henny Youngman

In the end, like most examples of female-demeaning behavior, the JAP joke is much more a reflection of and comment upon the position of the Jewish male joke teller.

While, for the most part, we see much of Jewish humor rooted in the cultural commonalities of the universal human experience, there's no denying Jeremy Dauber's claim that, both philosophically and psychologically, Jewish comedy is a direct response to a long history of persecution and anti-Semitism. Other national groups and religions have been, of course, pilloried and persecuted, and there is no sense in trying to measure which group has suffered more. As Dave Chappelle puts it, you "can't do comparative suffering. . . . Black people know about comparative suffering, and you know that it's a fucking dead-end game. Blacks and Jews do that shit to each other all the time. You ever played 'Who Suffered More' with a Jewish person? It's a tough game. Whenever you think you've got the Jewish guy on the ropes, that motherfucker will be like, 'Well don't forget about Egypt.'"[7] There's no sense in trying to claim Jews have been more persecuted. What is important is that the historical tradition, varied experience, and transcontextual nature of Jewish persecution is sui generis. Have you read the Old Testament lately?

When you think about it, it is perhaps not surprising that the development and popularization of great American art, and especially satirical and comedic art—stand-up comedy, the Broadway musical, jazz, the comic strip—correspond with both the great migration of blacks escaping Jim Crow from the South to northern cities and larger influxes of Jews to America. Both groups have historically been excluded from, while remaining within earshot of, mainstream society—giving them the insider's familiarity as well as the outsider's critical point of view. This perhaps explains why African Americans and Jews have had such a disproportionate degree of artistic, literary, and cultural influence: they inherit the historical and social position to mock the Serious Ones in the language of those deemed unserious, nurtured in segregated enclaves (whether the Chitlin' Circuit or the borscht belt) that functioned as cultural incubators. Among the great American comedians and satirists, it is the WASPs who are in the minority. Carlin sits relatively alone among the Pryors, Seinfelds, Murphys, Bruces, Macs, Dangerfields, Allens, and so on. Bill Pullman might have been the president in *Independence Day*, but he needed Will Smith and Jeff Goldblum to fly the spaceship.

So, what constitutes an authentic response to generation after generation of dehumanization, international abuse, spontaneous violence, local pogroms, and government-sponsored genocide? What's the answer to the questions "If we're the chosen people, what's the deal?" and "Why did you have to choose us? A new day it may be, but oy, oy, oy, the same old troubles keep happening without remission or relief."[8] After a while, it's hard to keep up the pretense that it isn't personal. Many Jews come to the unfortunate conclusion that God can be something of a letdown. For example:

An old Jew, who prays at the Western Wall, is known to have been going there to pray every day, many times a day, for many years.

An enterprising young American reporter is told about the old man and his hours of daily praying. Believing it might make a good human-interest story, the reporter goes to the wall, and, sure enough, there is the old man bent in prayer. After watching the old Jew pray for about an hour and a half, and then seeing him slowly walk away, cane in hand, the reporter approaches him and asks him his name. The old Jew answers that his name is Irving Rabinowitz. The reporter then inquires how long Mr. Rabinowitz has been praying at the Western Wall, and Rabinowitz pauses and answers, "Sixty-seven years."

"That is remarkable," says the young reporter. "What do you pray for?" Rabinowitz says that he prays for peace between Jews, Muslims, and Christians and for the love of human beings for their fellow humans. He adds that he also prays for politicians to be honest. At this point, the reporter asks, "So, what has it been like for you praying all these years?" Rabinowitz answers, "It's like talking to a fucking wall."

Or, as Woody Allen succinctly and stoically put it, "I don't think that He's [God] evil. I think the worst you can say about Him is that, basically, He's an underachiever!"[9]

What to do? Or, to paraphrase Spinoza, "Whither shall I turn with my anguish and complaint?" The answer: Joking in the face of horror. Humor as an antidote to suffering. Comedy as a response to pointless tragedy. Mirth to combat the murder and madness of it all. Laughter as a celebration of survival. The communion of laughter with others. Hence, the classic universal comic toast for all Jewish holidays:

They tried to kill us!
    They didn't!
    Let's eat!

Ironically, it can be argued that the zeitgeist of Jewish humor and comedy indirectly and unintentionally mirrors the convoluted writings of an accused anti-Semite and perhaps the gloomiest and least happy of all philosophers, Friedrich Nietszche: "We possess art lest we perish from the truth."[10]

Truth is often hard to bear. Truth that is difficult or ugly is impossible to bear. We need the art of humor to make the truths of life (the good, the bad, and the ugly) more bearable. Humor, like art, softens the blows of reality. Humor gives us another way of looking at things.

Another way of interpreting reality. Another way to mitigate the inevitable.

The philosopher, theologian, and occasional stand-up comic Mel Brooks is our one true rabbi (teacher) in this matter. Brooks contends that in "days of old," for every ten Jews God created, he designed one to be a comic to both entertain and distract the others. Otherwise, says Brooks, the collective wailing and lamentations of the Israeli tribe would have been unbearable.[11] We need humor, says Brooks, "as a defense against the Universe"; we need humor "to fight off the given as well as our fear of the unknown, the unanswerable, and the unacceptable."[12] Or, in the words of a fictitious Jewish comedian, Miriam Maisel, from Amazon Prime's *The Marvelous Mrs. Maisel*, "Comedy is fueled by depression, sadness, despair, or the lack of other alternatives."[13]

For Brooks, humor offers us a timeout, a reprieve, a mechanism to disarm the moment and/or, at the very least, keep reality at bay. Comedy, joke telling offers us a way to deal with some of the unavoidable absurdities, complexities, and paradoxes of life. When we laugh at one of life's mysteries, cruelties, or horrors, we diminish (if only temporarily) its terror in our imagination. Joke telling offers us a window into the unknowable and the irresolvable. Jokes about sex, marriage, children, money, illness, death, religion, and God may not provide definitive answers, but they can alleviate some of our fears, afford comfort and distraction, and perhaps, just perhaps, offer us some perspective, some illumination with regard to these fundamentally irresolvable and yet unavoidable issues. Jokes allow us to disarm reality and not be defeated by it. Humor, jokes, and laughter can act as both a sword and a shield to defend ourselves against life. At least for a while, humor can detox the mysteries and make the unknown, the intolerable, and the utterly unavoidable more bearable.

But, Brooks is quick to point out, "there is a difference" between silly comedy ("fart jokes" like the cowboy bean dinner scene in *Blazing Saddles*) and serious humor as captured in the big production number of his multi-Emmy Award–winning play and film *The Producers*, "Springtime for Hitler and Germany." Brooks argues that *The Producers* is a comedic vehicle that allows us to laugh at, belittle, and cast shame on everything that Hitler and the Nazi Party stood for. "*The Producers* is my revenge. My comedic goal was to defeat Nazism," said Brooks. "When we laugh at them we win through ridicule. . . . It's a Jewish way of getting through it, getting over it. We get the last laugh."[14] It's not denial. It's not sublimation. It's a way of spitting in the face of fate.

Etgar Keret, Israeli humorist and novelist, agrees with Brooks and argues that humor is often the "only weapon of the weak." Comedy allows us, at least for a while, to push back, to be contrarians. And, sometimes, it allows us to vanquish our demons.[15]

One of the most famous survivors of the Holocaust was psychiatrist and philosopher Viktor Frankl, who endured almost four years of hard labor at Auschwitz. Frankl quickly learned that without "choosing" to find some humor in the midst of the misery of the camps, life was not bearable or survivable. He learned that laughter affords us an aloofness and ability to rise above any situation, even if only for a few seconds. Without those few moments, said Frankl, "I would never had made it."[16]

It's certainly not the case that prisoners in these concentration camps greeted each other at roll call by saying, "Hey, did you hear the one about . . . ?" Nor did they sit over their eight ounces of rancid gruel each night and swap nasty and satirical Nazi stories. Rather, said Frankl, inmates tried to use their imaginations to create or see humor in any situation possible. For example, there is the story of a prisoner who points to a particularly severe and sadistic capo (a prisoner who served as guard) and ironically says to a fellow inmate, "Imagine! I knew him when he was only the president of a bank!"[17]

German historian Rudolph Herzog maintains that these kinds of jokes are an expression of the Jewish prisoner's desire to survive against all odds. Such jokes are a desperate attempt to deny, if only momentarily, the everyday terror of the camps. For Herzog, these jokes are an act of defiance: "My back is to the wall, [but] I'm still laughing." These jokes are proof that the speaker is not dead yet: "I laugh, therefore I still am!" Laughing in the face of a nightmare does not enable one to wake from it suddenly, but somehow it becomes, at least briefly, just a bit more endurable.[18] As one survivor said, "Even when you were laughing through your tears, it's still laughter. It was the only weapon we had in the ghetto."[19]

In a wonderful but little-known documentary, *When Comedy Went to School*, six Jewish comics—Jerry Lewis, Sid Caesar, Larry King, Robert Klein, Jackie Mason, and Jerry Stiller—reminisce about what they learned about the importance of comedy while performing in the Catskill Jewish resorts after World War II. Besides learning their craft—two or three shows a night, seven days a week—they learned the role of humor/comedy in the lives of their audiences. As Jackie Mason suggested, they were eager to laugh; they wanted to laugh. The war was over. Laughing was a way of saying, "We survived." Jokes were payback—their only revenge.[20]

Jews jest because they are not amused. Because there are no other viable options. Perhaps being a Jew means that life requires you to be a "militant comedic contrarian."

History has taught the children of Abraham to be "on guard," cautious, skeptical, and distrustful of the world. Even in the good times, when life is not cruel, it is always hard, a struggle. Individually and as a people, Jews have alternatively used humor as a narcotic, a tool, a weapon, and a buffer to seek relief, acceptance, or stoical resignation regarding the triumphs and vicissitudes of life. As many Jewish scholars have correctly pointed out, "Humor is seldom the only answer." But what humorlessness fails to recognize is just how useful humor can be in confronting what one finds offensive, intolerable, or beyond comprehension. In the words of Chicago-based comedian Aaron Freeman, "I don't just tell jokes to earn a living or just because they are funny—I tell jokes as a self-defense mechanism."[21]

CHAPTER 6

A Debate on the Ethics of Offensive Comedy

"Lighten up and don't worry about the words comedians use. . . . We gotta stop policing comedians. This is America."

—ANDREW DICE CLAY

We are in the midst of what many consider a "comedy boom." The proliferation of media and venues for comedians has corresponded with an increase in comedic performers and audiences. It has also meant an increase in critical commentary on comedy. One of the ongoing topics of conversation among comics, critics, and consumers is whether comedians "go too far" or veer too far into offensive territory. Some comedians—Dave Chappelle, Joe Rogan, Jerry Seinfeld, and Steve Harvey, among many others—have claimed that in spite of the increase in interest (and money) for comedians, it is also a dangerous time for comedy because of audiences' increased sensitivity. Others insist that this so-called increased sensitivity is actually just called "being enlightened" and is a good thing, enabling comedy to be more inclusive of and sensitive to various audience groups.

The purpose of this chapter is to explore questions at the heart of this debate. How do you decide whether a particular joke is ethical or unethical? How do we decide if the joke should be told at all? To put this subject in the language that people like to use in these conversations, must comedians avoid "punching down," or can they make their jokes without the constraints of such social and ethical considerations?

On the topic of the ethics of joke telling and whether jokes should or should not be told for social, political, or racial reasons, we are a house divided. One of us (Gini) would argue that although we give comics a huge amount of social/cultural latitude and license to push the envelope, there is a point at which good taste, civility, and ethics require that certain kinds of jokes not be told. However, one of us (Singer) believes that any joke and any topic is potentially fair game—no matter how crude, off putting, vulgar, insensitive, or offensive—as long as the comic has the craft, talent, and timing to sell it to the audience.

Instead of trying to find some mushy middle ground wherein we find a staid and boring consensus, we have decided to stage this chapter as a trial. For the prosecution, Gini will present the case against offensive comedy, arguing that there is a topical line that comedians ought not cross. For the defense, Singer will argue that such standards are inevitably unworkable and that the ethics of comedy is actually quite a bit subtler and more difficult than often thought.

FOR THE PROSECUTION

Let me (Gini) start by looking at a few basics. Jokes and satire are stories or short descriptive narratives based on fiction or fact that are intended to amuse, delight, and possibly inform. All jokes are, to some degree or another, edgy, irreverent, iconoclastic, or off putting. In making fun of somebody or something, jokes push the conventional verbal, conceptual, and cultural envelope. This means that every joke has the potential to offend someone or to be an affront to something. Every piece of humor risks goring someone's sacred cow. "Language is never neutral." It's all about proper "context." Everything is potentially funny.[1] The initial issue being advocated here is not whether a joke is ethically correct or ethically objectionable. Rather, the issue is this: How is it possible that an utterly tasteless joke, a joke that many consider crude, rude, inappropriate, highly offensive, and even harmful, can be considered funny? To begin to answer this question, we need to briefly examine the four basic elements involved in joke telling.

I. The teller	The joker
II. The tale	The joke
III. The timing	The moment
IV. The told	The audience

I.   *The teller.* Like any good salesperson, the joker needs to sell him- or herself as well as the joke or comedic bit. Whether the joke is delivered by a professional onstage or by a friend over dinner, more often than not, jokes succeed or fail depending upon how well they are presented. Getting a laugh at a comedy club or at a neighbor's kitchen table is as much a trick of timing, pacing, and delivery as it is a demonstration of true wit.[2]

II. *The tale.* The joke itself has to be interesting or clever, or unusual or unexpected, or profound or profane, or something that arrests, shocks, surprises, delights, or disgusts the intended audience. According to writer, director, actor, and comic Mel Brooks, "Comedy must be daring. It must skirt the edge of bad taste. If it doesn't, it's not challenging or exciting—or funny."[3]

III. *The timing.* Timing is much more than pacing the delivery of the joke. Timing, in a larger sense, is about the appropriateness of the joke in the moment. Timing and circumstance can never be overlooked. Every comic and joke teller needs to determine when it is appropriate to tell a particular joke. When is the joke too soon? When is the subject matter too close for comfort? When is it too distant to matter? Where's the sweet spot? When is it too raw, too horrifying, and too undigested to make fun of?

IV. *The told.* In the end, more important than the teller or the timing, the joke itself, the tale, only has viability if it has currency with the told. That is, does the audience think it's funny? Just as the three ironclad rules of real estate are "location, location, location," a successful joke or piece of satire is all about "audience, audience, audience." The life cycle of a humorous statement is like the physics of sound. A noise must be emitted and received for the circuit to be completed and for sound to occur.

What this means is that "all jokes are conditional"— that is, all jokes have conditional requirements connecting the teller and the audience, or common knowledge, common background, common language, and common cultural presuppositions, prejudices, and myths. When a joke works, it's because the joker is telling a story and using assumptions, knowledge, cultural references, and a background that an audience recognizes, understands, and can react and respond to. The most elemental reason why jokes do not work is because we do not all share the same life experiences, the same frames of reference. In the end, we are a society divided by different tastes because we are a society of different backgrounds and experiences. The conditional nature of joke telling explains why jokes, comics, music, and comedy are so subjective, community specific, generational, or niche based.[4] As Northrop Frye has suggested, satire and all of comedy require wit, an object of attack or point of reference, and an attuned, intelligent audience.[5]

Pushed to its logical conclusion, what this means is that nasty jokes, naughty jokes, nefarious jokes, sexual jokes, misogynistic jokes, racial jokes, antireligious jokes, scatological jokes (no matter how graphic, crude, perverse, despicable, and derogatory) can, depending on the tastes and receptivity of the audience, be considered acceptable fodder for comedy—in other words, be considered funny! No matter how counterintuitive it may seem, that some or many might deem a joke offensive, vulgar, or even unethical doesn't mean that the joke is aesthetically flawed and not funny to a particular audience. As philosopher and joke guru Ted Cohen somewhat reluctantly insists, "Do not let your convictions that a joke is in bad taste, or downright immoral, blind you to whether you find it funny." Ethics, common sense, and good taste aside, the humor of a joke depends absolutely upon who tells the joke and who hears it.[6]

Let's be very clear about this point: I'm not talking about jokes that "might" offend Emily Post's refined standards or aesthetic sensibility and good taste. Or jokes you probably shouldn't tell your mother. I'm talking about jokes that intentionally, happily push the limits of sadomasochism. Jokes that far exceed playful childhood scatology. Jokes that are positively gleeful about necrophilia, cannibalism, and torture. Jokes that viciously diminish, denigrate, and defame the basic human rights of various political, racial, or ethnic groups. Jokes that celebrate misogyny or advocate violence, mutilation, even death. We need to ask, even if the audience thinks jokes like this are funny, are they ethical? Should they be told?

For a lot of people, comedy simply transcends the usual cultural and moral norms. "C'mon," people will say, "it's just a joke." Or "Calm down, jokes let us cross the line on any issue." In theory, in a perfect world, perhaps. But as Emily Nussbaum of the *New Yorker* has noted, the phrase "Can't you take a joke?" is too often code for justifying sexism, racism, and/or the expression of a prejudicial point of view of your choosing.[7] "It's just a joke" can be used as a flimsy excuse to justify perhaps technically funny but nevertheless unethical jokes about rape, race, homophobia, sexism, and so forth.

Many people claim that joke telling is cathartic and can disarm and dismantle various stereotypes and prejudices and level the playing field for all concerned. But not always. In fact, it can be argued that it is "virtually impossible to make a joke about racism or sexism that isn't also a racist, sexist joke." Ironically, in trying to "defang" a sensitive topic, joking can inadvertently normalize and entrench racism or any prejudicial point of view rather than neutralize or negate it. The danger in telling "funny" racist jokes is that we run the risk of perpetuating them and the negative ideas that they reflect. Case in point: Chris Rock. In 1996, Rock was on tour and performing a routine titled "N****** vs. Black People." After the tour, he never performed it again because he was convinced he was giving his white audience permission and license to use the N-word.[8]

Until November 2017, when Louis C.K. was forced to stand down from his stand-up career after admitting to inappropriate sexual conduct, he was arguably Jerry Seinfeld's successor as the "King of Comedy." What Louis C.K. did onstage was not tell jokes so much as analyze, criticize, and satirize—marriage, divorce, raising kids, loneliness, being rich versus being poor, or why he likes being a white guy. As one commentator succinctly put it, "Louis C.K. is edgy and a little scary too. He takes

only a fucking psychopath would think like that, and
the simplicity of the joke lays that bare.[11]

Sorry, I don't buy it. I think that this joke is a "bridge too far." It may, in fact, be funny, but I think that it's unethical. I think it pushes the limits of good taste and civilized discourse too far.

In mid-December 2018, Louis C.K., as part of the process of redeeming himself and making a comeback, booked a six-performance gig at a Long Island comedy club. According to media reports, C.K.'s set included disparaging remarks about Asians, poked fun at teenagers who were gender neutral or confused about the exact nature of their own sexuality, and made a sexually explicit joke about a nine-year-old girl. And what I (Gini) found most shocking was his vitriolic comments regarding the survivors of the February 2018 massacre at Marjory Stoneman Douglas High School in Parkland, Florida, in which seventeen teenagers and adults were killed.

They testify in front of Congress, these kids. You're not interesting 'cause you went to a high school where kids got shot. Why does that mean I have to listen to you? How does that make you interesting? You didn't get shot. You put some fat kid in the way and now I gotta listen to you talking?[12]

According to Scott Simon, on NPR's *Weekend Edition*, "Great comics can be offensive and outrageous in their acts, but they have to be funny." He found nothing funny but a great deal that was offensive in C.K.'s act. Simon's concluding comments on this story reflect my own views on the matter: "A comic who dares to be offensive, but isn't funny, is just a lout!"[13]

Humor is not a pardon, a passport, or a get-out-of-jail-free card that lets you say anything. "You just didn't get it" is never a sufficient or satisfactory excuse to justify or explain away a malevolent or vicious comedic zinger. The use of humor does not insulate us, isolate us, disengage us, or detach us from our basic responsibilities to and relationships with others. Intentionally laughing at or callously ridiculing the misfortunes of others, laughing at or about who they are, the color of their skin, or their particular personal circumstances, is reprehensible, destructive, and unethical. Comedy can be boisterous, biting, iconoclastically satirical, shocking, off putting, and probing. But it need not and should not be degrading, derogatory, dehumanizing, and/or poignantly unethical. It, especially, need not be personally "ugly."

Social theorist Arthur Koestler has argued that a consistent scornful and contemptuous style of humor is, in essence, contempt for all things unfamiliar and a "defensive antidote to sympathy."[14] It can also be argued that the persistent pattern of derogatory humor is a demonstration of deep-seated aggression, fear, and rage. I (Gini) couldn't agree more.

FOR THE DEFENSE

Now that the prosecution has rested its case against certain sorts of jokes and humor, I (Singer) find myself in the unenviable position of rising in their defense. The prosecutor, Al Gini, has presented his case for what we can call "the conventional wisdom." The conventional wisdom goes something like this:

> *There are certain things that one simply shouldn't joke about. Of course, comedians get to be rude, irreverent, and indecent. We're not the arresters of Lenny Bruce or the Tipper Gores of yesteryear. But that doesn't mean they get to say anything. Comedians have an ethical obligation when delivering jokes, particularly to avoid reinforcing biased social perceptions of particular groups and the unequal power dynamics of our unjust society.*

Making such jokes is wrong, the conventional wisdom says, not because it offends our sense of decorum or the moral fiber of our society but because it contributes to harm and injustice.

This point often gets summed up in an ethical maxim that comedians are advised to follow, which we might call the "Punch up" rule: Comedians should train their sights on the privileged who benefit from current injustice and inequality. But they also must avoid making fun of those who don't.

It's a powerful view that has much to recommend it. And yet I wish to stand in defense of offensive comedy against this conventional wisdom, even comedy that might be accused of contributing to harm and injustice. Comedic speech is radically different from other forms of speech. As a consequence, comedy comes with very different standards of moral rightness and wrongness. In general, we ought to be far more modest, humble, and reserved in our moral judgment of comedy, including comedy we find politically and socially problematic. I want to argue that comedians may, in principle, *punch anywhere*, though this will be limited by the concerns of their craft and their audiences.

We should start by trying to understand why the question of ethics and comedy is so difficult. Why isn't the answer simply "What's immoral or wrong to say off-stage is immoral or wrong to say onstage?"

One way of thinking about this topic is to think of comedy as being governed by what moral theorists sometimes refer to as "role ethics." Within a society, people occupy special kinds of positions that empower them to act in ways we normally would discourage or disallow. We grant football players permission to tackle other football players; in everyday life we call this "assault," but on the football field it's called a "sack." We grant police officers permission to use force in ways not available to rest of us. Fire truck and ambulance drivers are allowed to drive in ways that would get the rest of our licenses suspended. We like to think of society as governed by general standards of morality. But when we look at it more closely, we see that we actually grant a lot of exemptions to everyday morality in order to allow people to do tasks we as a society see as valuable.

But this doesn't mean that such positions are devoid of morality. Quite the contrary. Police officers are permitted to do things most aren't, but they are also supposed to be held to various professional and legal standards when doing so. Boxers and football players can engage in violent activity in ways normal citizens can't, but only in certain circumstances, and still within the bounds of sportsmanship. Emergency vehicles can break certain laws of the road that other citizens cannot, but they also don't get to stop at the drive-thru window on a whim in the way other motorists can. Lawyers are required to zealously defend despicable people but also have various sorts of professional ethical codes they have to live up to. (OK, maybe lawyers aren't the best example.)

Our societies create various roles that people occupy in order to accomplish socially valuable things: entertaining sports, law and order, speedy emergency responses, a functioning economy, a legal system, and so forth. These roles often come with certain exemptions from standard morality but also with certain moral restrictions that don't apply to the rest of us. This is what moral and political theorists refer to as "role ethics."

Comedy works in a similar way. We allow comedians to do all sorts of things that everyday morality and decorum disallow or frown upon: being an attention hog and dominating the conversation, being irreverent, making fun of people, saying offensive things, breaking taboos, and so forth. But we do this in the service of a certain end: to provide entertainment, to make people laugh, and (as we have argued) to encourage the sorts of insights and dispositions that are crucial for the health, stability, and progress of society.

If we look at comedians this way—as filling a special role or social office with distinct privileges and responsibilities—then our moral assessment of comedy becomes different. Of course, some general moral prohibitions apply to comedians like they do to anybody— comedians (like all people) must avoid, say, incitements of violence. However, other times, our normal moral codes don't apply to comedians: comedians are allowed to be rude and offensive in ways the rest of us are not.

Even more to the point, comedians are allowed to have a more playful and lax attitude toward the truth, such that "don't lie" or "don't slander" are obviously not applicable to the joker.

We can't just think of morality in general when it comes to comedy. Kant's categorical imperative or Aristotle's golden mean cannot help us here. No, if we want to think about the ethics of comedy, we have to ask something subtler: What are the moral codes specific to comedy and inherent in the role of "comedian"?

This is what "Punch up" is an answer to. The claim that comedians ought to "punch up" is acknowledging that comedians have special privileges (namely, "punching") but that this comes with the specific obligation to direct their hardened fists at those with power and not at the marginalized. "Punch up" takes seriously the idea that the comedian has a special kind of role, to which special sorts of ethical considerations are attached. The idea underlying "Punch up" is that, of course, comedy is going to involve offending groups and hurting people's feelings. However, the license given to the comedian to offend and mock comes with the special responsibility to do so in a specific way: with social awareness and a responsibility not to harm the already harmed or marginalize the already marginalized. Thus, joke tellers must take care not to punch down and make jokes at the expense of those who already bear the brunt of social inequality.

It's a powerful idea. But there are at least three problems with the idea of "Punch up." First, it is not always clear which way "up" is. Second, it's not always clear when a comedian is actually "punching." And third, the moral guideline actually becomes self-defeating when put into practice.

First, to the idea of "Punch up," we can ask, "Which way is up?" The idea of punching up is based on the view that societies are always marked by power, which puts some people "up" on the top and others "down" at the bottom. What makes this idea complicated, though, is that society is marked by a number of different interlocking power dynamics that pull in different directions.[15] One person may be "up" on the basis of class but still "down" when looked at through the lens of racial hierarchy or gender identification. Such facts are amplified when we note that power dynamics within a city are not the same as those within a country or those within a global order. A religious group might be a subjugated minority within a small town but part of a powerful majority when looked at in national or global terms.

As an example, think of *Charlie Hebdo*, the controversial satirical French magazine that was the victim of a horrific mass shooting. *Hebdo* was often criticized for engaging in Islamophobic comedy, especially by virtue of its infamous covers, which often featured childish cartoon drawings of Mohammad engaging in sex acts or in other positions that devout Muslims would find offensive or heretical. As many critics put it, *Charlie Hebdo* was "punching down" by mocking Islamic practices, given the marginal status and widespread maltreatment of Muslims in French society. This appeared to be the view of Gary Trudeau, arguably America's greatest satirical cartoonist. In contrast to his fellow cartoonists who rushed to the support of *Hebdo* in response to the violence, Trudeau criticized the French satirical outfit along very familiar lines: "By punching downward, by attacking a powerless, disenfranchised minority with crude, vulgar drawings closer to graffiti than cartoons, *Charlie [Hebdo]* wandered into the realm of hate speech."[16]

Trudeau here sounds like a "Punch up" acolyte, criticizing *Hebdo* for punching down. As we will see later, I actually think Trudeau's view is subtler than that—even if he doesn't realize it. But for now, this statement captures a common perception of *Hebdo*: though undeserving of such violent attack, the satirical outfit was still guilty of punching down.

I admit to not finding *Hebdo*'s covers terribly funny or clever. However, I also think that judging whether they were "punching down" is not so simple. As people defending *Hebdo* pointed out, criticizing Islamic extremism could be considered punching up against a powerful force in world politics (even if, within France, Muslims are marginalized). This was, it must be noted, *Hebdo*'s claim. The offense taken by French Muslims notwith-standing, *Hebdo* always claimed its jabs were aimed at the extremist and intolerant faction of Muslim extrem-ists, who do exercise power in certain parts of the world and in geopolitics more broadly. That Muslims in France took offense, according to *Hebdo*, was unfortunate but not the intent—they were aiming to punch not down but up at a particular powerful and immoral group of people.

The horrific shootings at *Hebdo*'s offices were, in some tragic sense, grist for *Hebdo*'s mill. The "punch" (whether upward or downward) of the cartoonist's pen seems to pale in comparison to that of gunfire and spilled blood. Is a comedian really punching down when his or her targets respond to metaphorical barbs with real bul-lets and bombs? We have to note that the violent attack on *Hebdo* was pretty effective in certain respects. Trudeau criticized *Hebdo*, citing the violence as being caused by its hate speech, as many others did. However, *Hebdo* had been producing its covers for years before the attack, and I can't find evidence of Trudeau criticizing the magazine until afterward. Not only did the violence result in death and murder, but it also popularized a particular view of *Charlie Hebdo* and the unacceptability of its satire.

None of this means that *Hebdo* was totally blameless for its satire. But it does point to an interesting question: What sorts of power do comedians exercise, and what sorts of power are they are vulnerable to? When people criticize a comedian for punching down, it's almost always in reference to the comedian's class, gender, race, ability, or nationality. It's rarely in terms of the fact that the person is, in this instance, taking on the role of a comedian. Where does the comic, *as a comic*, fit in intersectional webs of power?

It's a tough question that resists easy answers. Successful comedians obviously have a sort of privilege and platform that few of us have—particularly in commanding the attention and influencing the perspectives of audiences. This position certainly must come with responsibility.

However, comedians are also subject to a kind of scrutiny and criticism that few of us are. This is not just as performers and celebrities but specifically as comedians. If satire involves pointing out the absurdity of the serious and self-assured, this means that comedians and satirists will always be uniquely vulnerable to the blowback of the sanctimonious and offended. Because comedians puncture the sacred truths and expectations that we cling to, they are always in danger of offending a group who will feel that the comedian hasn't simply "offended" them but harmed or defied something true that they hold dear.

Satirists are always in a precarious position. They are always subject to the sensibilities of the self-righteous and slighted. And these offended parties often, in their self-righteousness, enlist other sources of power—religion, social conformity and sanction, government, or armed violence—and respond disproportionately to the perceived offense.

This doesn't get comedians entirely off the hook, of course. I am not claiming that comedians *as comedians* are comparable to marginalized classes of racial, gender, sexual, or religious groups in terms of the powers to which they are subject. Still, comedians face pressures and potential harms that are specific to their activities, making this sort of sociopolitical analysis more difficult than it seems.

This is one basic complication for the idea of "Punch up": it's often hard to know which way is "up" in a complex, interconnected, and multifaceted world, where people are liable to miscomprehend their position and respond disproportionately to perceived harms. Of course, there are many times when we can clearly identify the robber baron or the gentrifier as "up" in contrast to the "down"-trodden evicted family or exploited worker. Other times, though, the world looks less like a pyramid and more like a dogpile, where it is difficult to tell which dog is the "underdog." Given that, it is not always clear which way is up and which way is down when we're punching—or when we're getting punched.

A second problem with "Punch up" is that figuring out what really counts as a "punch" is itself often difficult. One of the annoying side effects of moralizing about comedy or looking for the social responsibility in the joke is that it tends to do so at the expense of recognizing when something is funny. Read the text of any joke as if it were just a prose paragraph, and it comes across as disjointed and unfunny—but it can also come across as mean or dismissive, despite how it seemed in delivery. In describing how his previous comedy routines were weaponized against him on the campaign trail, Al Franken (the comedian-turned-senator-turned-disgraced-ex-senator) once described opponents as using the "DeHumorizer," an expensive machine designed "to take out any context or irony or hyperbole or anything, to make anything I had said or written in thirty-eight years of comedy horrible."[17] This tactic is so effective because jokes are unique in how they work and are not like other political statements.

With the exception of the most schticky Vegas acts or the most sterile Bob Hope–era comedians, almost all comedians employ heavy doses of irony and sarcasm in their acts. Sometimes, oftentimes, the bad thing being said about the homeless, or Jews, or Congress is being said not earnestly but in jest. There is an unstated understanding—to state it, after all, would be to "explain" the joke, and nothing is less funny than that—that what comedians are saying isn't really what they are *saying*. Just as often, they are making fun of, or making light of, the position they are pretending to take.

Sometimes comedians are not taking a position on the topic at all but using it as a way to make fun of themselves or to point at some broader absurdity. Taking a joke at face value and assessing the offensiveness of what a comedian is "saying" almost always misses this point—it treats a comedy routine as a confessional, an editorial column, or a policy platform.

Gini brought up the infamous Louis C.K. Parkland shooting routine in his section. I think in doing this, my esteemed and learned coauthor may have fallen into the DeHumorizer trap. If we take C.K.'s statement out of context and at face value, then of course it is an unconscionably cruel and mean thing to say. While I don't wish to fully defend C.K. here, I think the context does change the meaning of the joke quite a bit. The setup to the joke is C.K. talking about how wild and immature he was as a teenager and how offensive his behavior was to his parents. He had expected, at this age, to be shocked and scandalized by current teenagers' behavior. Instead, he sees socially conscious and politically engaged people changing the way they speak and actively lobbying Congress. The ridicule isn't meant to be genuine but is instead a sort of self-mockery—noting how dumb his generation was in comparison—or just a note about how different today's youth is when compared to previous generations. The anger and over-the-top resentment are meant to bring this point out with ironic effect.

This isn't to say it's a good joke—far from it. The point here is just that taking the context of a joke seriously changes how you view it. I don't think C.K.'s joke was terribly funny (I'll return to this point later). But there are many "meanings" one can glean from it, which differ greatly from the one that most criticized him for.

Jokes generally don't have one discrete meaning. They are often meant to work at different levels and sometimes don't have one clear or discernible message. Saying comedians must never punch down assumes there is one stable and discernible message in a joke—one target, which must be selected correctly.

Jokes are often told from quasi-fictional and exaggerated perspectives, personas, and premises. They rarely should be taken as a comedian's earnest perspective. This point is often difficult to remember because what good comedians do—particularly stand-up comedians—is *appear* earnest or sincerely opinionated in their routines. But comedians' jokes are more akin to magicians' card tricks or actors' monologues than op-ed columns. Because of this situation, what looks like a "punch down" is often more of a stage punch, meant to mimic a view without being a straightforward endorsement of it. How offensive such jokes are is not a function of the content of the joke but the craft and skill with which the comedian delivered it—how well the irony, the context, or the perspective was laid out to make the joke *funny*.

And this is the big point: I believe almost anything can be joked about as long as it is joked about well. Once we start moralizing about what comedians can rightfully joke about, we're not just in the business of protecting the powerless from the powerful—we're also in the business of blunting the tools of satire, removing topics and sensibilities from the table, even though in the right hands the jokes could be good and responsible. And this idea leads to the third problem with "Punch up": it is ultimately self-defeating.

Here's the thing about ideas: Sometimes they work! Sometimes people start to believe some ethical principle and then begin acting according to it. When enough people do so, the idea affects and alters cultures and the way societies behave. I don't think it's too far a stretch to suggest that "Punch up" has, in many circles, attained this status. People are censured, "cancelled," and shunned for punching down and being irresponsible in their jokes because "Punch up" has attained a certain position as the moral consensus, the correct way of doing comedy.

Whatever the merits might be of "Punch up," the problem is that once it becomes effective—once it gets comedians to think about their craft in one way as opposed to another, and once it gets critics and publics to like some comedians and not others—it exerts a kind of power. Indeed, that is the whole point. But what do comedians do to power? They mock it! They come for it and subject it to the deconstructing and disruptive force of satire!

The more persuasive the idea of "Punch up" becomes, the more enticing it is for many comedians to ridicule and undercut. The more people agree "Let's not make fun of *x*," the bigger the invitation becomes for comedians to transgress the norm and find a good angle on *x*! By this I don't mean that all comedians will automatically try to break taboos or that they should. Rather, I mean that the satirical sensibility sniffs out conventions, convictions, and widely held beliefs and holds them up for the sort of critical reflection that only humor can really allow.

This is as it should be. Satire exists precisely to disrupt the conventional wisdom, settled norms, and standards of good judgment. This aspect of satire doesn't become less important just because it challenges what we happen to believe is right, good, and obvious. Even our most well-meaning and best-considered attempts to protect people are always attempts to impose order on a messy and complicated social world. And it is this very presumptuous ambition that satirists take aim at. As comedian Jeremy McLellan once noted, "All art is necessarily problematic insofar as it bears witness to a reality that resists being solved."[18]

The problem with the idea that it is immoral or unjust to joke about certain topics, people, or things is that it simultaneously takes comedy too seriously and doesn't take it seriously enough! It takes comedy too seriously in not recognizing that jokes are not like other kinds of speech or utterances: covered in irony and sarcasm and situated within deliberate perspectives, they get their meaning and power as much from their timing, setup, and premise as from their literal semantic meaning. Holding comedy to a standard like "Punch up" is like criticizing professional wrestlers for assaulting one another—you can't analyze the punches, takedowns, or piledrivers outside of their context, whether that's the wrestling ring or the brick-backed stage at the Improv.

But the "Punch up" maxim also doesn't take comedy seriously enough! When we take topics off the table to joke about, we are inherently trying to exercise a sort of power over comedians. George Carlin once quipped, "Everyone appreciates your honesty . . . until you're honest with them. Then you're an asshole." If we take satire seriously, we must be willing to take ourselves, and our most treasured beliefs, less seriously. We must allow the jokers to come for us, even when we're convinced of our rightness and their wrongness. When we attempt to tame this process, our taming attempt must—and should— become the target of the comic eye.

This doesn't mean comedians have no ethical responsibilities. Let's return to Gary Trudeau. As I noted above, his criticism of *Charlie Hebdo* seems to put him in the camp of the "Punch up" crowd. But if we keep reading his speech, we see that even he can't fully endorse that view. Even in Trudeau's account, *Hebdo* wasn't obviously "punching down" as much as it was being tragically mis-interpreted as such, as it always maintained that it was targeting Muslim fanatics, not Muslims tout court. Fur-thermore, Trudeau notes that throughout his career he's been the subject of criticism and blame for crossing the "red line" of acceptable satire. He tacitly acknowledges that "Punch up" is not always so obvious or easy to follow.

And so Trudeau ends with what I think is actually the best piece of ethical advice: "It's not easy figuring out where the red line is for satire anymore. But it's always worth asking this question: Is anyone, anyone at all, laughing? If not, maybe you crossed it." The punch-ing-up and -down language is gone here—we don't figure out where the red line of satire is by trying to identify the powerful and powerless or anything like that. Instead, Trudeau asks us to ask ourselves a simple question: "Is it funny?"

That, I think, is actually the morality of comedy. Be funny. It's not "Punch up"; it's "Land your punchlines." Often punching down is wrong not because it's targeting the marginal or comforting the powerful but because it's not funny. Comedians can, in principle, joke about any-thing and anybody—but they have to do it in service of being funny.

Often when we think a joke is unethically offensive, what we're saying is that the offense was gratuitous. Peo-ple were mocked or made fun of for no good reason, or a comedian drew on boring and lazy stereotypes. We can criticize comedians for doing that sort of thing without trying to draw lines around what and whom they can joke about. The problem isn't *what* they are joking about but the fact that they are doing it poorly.

Like police officers deputized to carry weapons or surgeons licensed to put scalpels in our skin, comedians have an obligation to ply their trade with care. Drawing on a racist stereotype, or making fun of women, or whatever, just "to be edgy" is like a surgeon finishing her procedure by carving her initials in your arm. Comedians who engage in jokes that perpetuate oppression for the sake of being offensive and appealing to the lowest common denominator are like police officers who abuse force just to assert their authority. They unethically misuse a granted privilege. Comedians must exercise care and caution and use their offensiveness not necessarily in service of justice, per se, but in service of their craft. After all, the satirical craft is good for a polity, in all the ways we discussed in chapter 3.

This isn't to say that comedians don't ever cross lines. They do! The problem is that these lines are often hard to identify in advance. A comedian might make a joke thinking it will land, only to botch it and end up unfunnily mocking people who don't deserve to be mocked. Our criticisms of comedy should reflect this fact.

We must recognize that doing comedy well is hard. This rule applies especially for comedians who are still working on their material. Jokes take a long time to develop, not just in terms of writing but also in terms of figuring out how they work and how best to deliver them. This means that what a comedian delivers at, say, the Comedy Cellar, the Comedy Store, or Zanies is often a work in progress. And when comedians are dealing with sensitive or delicate material, a joke that bombs will often result in offense without the funny to justify it.

But these venues exist precisely for such risk taking to happen. Again, even here, some jokes are just gratuitous and unclever and can be dismissed as such. But if the joke is an earnest attempt to try something risky—not just risqué for the sake of being so—the appropriate response is to recognize that this is part of the process and not rush to judgment.

Of course, judgment will not always be easy, and opinions will differ. Take Michael Richards. The comedian famous for playing Kramer on *Seinfeld* fell from grace in spectacular fashion when a tape leaked of him repeatedly referring to a black audience member as a "nigger." Now, I think there is some context in which a white comedian might effectively use this word in a routine. But this was not one of those instances: Richards quite obviously crossed the line.

Dave Chappelle, however, had a different take. Upon seeing the Richards blowup, Chappelle quipped that he learned something about himself: "You know what I learned? I learned that I'm only 20% black and 80% comedian.... The black dude in me was like 'Kramer, you motherfucker!' I was hurt! And the comedian in me was like 'nigga was having a bad set. Hang in there Kramer! Don't let 'em break you Kramer!'"[19] It's a great joke, but part of it is premised on Chappelle's acknowledgment that he can identify with what Richards was trying to do, even if he ultimately failed in the most devastating way possible.

Let's return to Louis C.K.'s Parkland joke for a moment. I think it's fair to criticize C.K. for the joke, but largely because he was dealing with sensitive material and didn't land the joke. It just wasn't funny enough to warrant the offense. In part this is because of how his position had changed in the public eye. C.K. was famous for being able to say basically anything onstage (this is, after all, the man who once said during his *SNL* monologue that pedophilia "must be really good" if pedophiles keep doing it!) and not only get away with it but also be praised by progressive circles. This was because people took him to be good and therefore baked that position into the premises of his jokes.

But when C.K. delivered the Parkland joke, it was after his sexual misconduct had been revealed and made public. With a change in his public perception came a change in how his jokes worked—or didn't work. But that's on him to know—the fact that the audience sees C.K. differently from how they did before isn't a good defense of the joke. The audience—broadly understood, not just the people who happen to be in the room—is the barometer, and if the joke doesn't land, it's on the comedian. The best defense for that joke was that it was delivered in a small club and was not being presented as finished or fully worked out. It was in the process of being developed and was leaked prematurely. Critics probably should have respected that a bit more than they did.

But this doesn't mean that comedians should get off scot-free either. If you listen to enough podcasts about comedy, you'll hear a number of comedians decrying how dangerous it is to be a comic these days and how awful the "sensitivity police" and "woke culture" are. While I understand where they are coming from, such comedians are trying to have their cake and eat it too. Comedy is a high-wire act. Part of what is so amazing about it when done well is that we all recognize how dangerous it is. Think about how we react to a really good comedian: "Oh man, I can't believe she said that!" "That's *aw*ful!" We are laughing both at the quality of the joke and at the recognition that in the wrong hands it wouldn't have worked—that we would never be able to do it.

Comedians who complain about the sensitivities of the audience are taking advantage of those sensitivities to get their laughs and then turning around and getting upset when it doesn't go their way. It's like the tightrope walker who missteps and then gets angry at gravity for being so cruel. The danger is part of the act and what makes it effective. The potential to mess up is part of the comedic effect and part of why audiences come in the first place.

Comedians get to try to make their jokes and get to make them about basically anything if they can pull it off. But if and when they miss and mess up, they don't get to blame the audience for not finding it funny. With the comedic license comes the responsibility to own your mistakes and take the blame when your jokes don't land. When their punchlines end up just being gratuitous punches, comedians don't get to blame those who just got slapped in the face.

Chapter 7

Do We Joke Too Much?

"Comedy can often be more of an opiate than a comfort."

—Greg Wolcott

Humor, comedy, and joke telling come in many different forms and can be described in many ways. It's fun. It's comfort food. It's obscene. It's a sword and a shield. It's urbane and philosophical. It's scandalous and inflammatory. It's slapstick and a pie in the face. Humor can also be a Band-Aid or a tourniquet, a cosmetic cover-up and/ or deep denial. But no matter how it's defined, used, or abused, we are in the midst of what many are calling a "golden age of comedy," while others have labeled it an "age of excessive comedy." The questions before us are (1) Which is which? and (2) Is this a good or a bad thing?

The modern origins and trajectory of our so-called golden age of comedy or age of excessive comedy follow a circuitous route, arguably starting with Mort Sahl and leading to Lenny Bruce to Richard Pryor to George Carlin, Eddie Murphy, and Chris Rock; to the Smothers

Brothers and then *Laugh-In*, the Comedy Store in Los Angeles, Gotham City Improv in New York, and Second City in Chicago; to *Saturday Night Live* and *The Simpsons* (longest-running TV sitcom in history); to *Real Time with Bill Maher*, to Jon Stewart and *The Daily Show*, to Stephen Colbert on *The Colbert Report*, to *Last Week Tonight* with Jon Oliver, to *Full Frontal* with Samantha Bee, and recently to *Patriot Act* with Hasan Minhaj, and the beat goes on and on!

Traditional nightclubs such as Mr. Kelly's in Chicago and the Copacabana in New York, as well as comedy clubs such as the Comedy Underground and the Purple Onion in San Francisco, have long been part of the American entertainment and comic tradition. But perhaps the major catalyst for our supposed golden age of comedy has been the explosion of small, privately owned and franchised comedy clubs such as Zanies, the Improv, and Uncle Vinnie's. These establishments are not copycat Second Cities or traditional nightclubs. They are clubs exclusively devoted to stand-up comedy. There's no band or dancing between acts. There are no musical interludes. It's usually just two comics—a headliner and a warm-up act—doing two to three sets a night. There's a cover charge, a two-drink minimum, and a not-so-funny reminder to "be sure to tip your server!"

On the home front, since the 1950s, the golden age of comedy has also been propelled and sustained by traditional network television and a long history of successful sitcoms, cable TV, HBO, and, more recently, various streaming services, which have propelled the success of the "comedy special" format.

The formula for these specials is very straightforward: a fairly well-known or up-and-coming comic talent, a large auditorium filled to the brim with paying and (more often than not) comped attendees, a basic three-camera shoot, good lighting, great sound, and, bingo, you are in show business. Netflix, HBO, Hulu, Amazon Prime, Showtime, Comedy Central, and Epix are all players in this game. On occasion, even staid and steady PBS gets a piece of the action. Besides television, of course, there's been a comedic explosion on the airwaves as well. Satellite radio has a number of channels dedicated to comedy. Even socially serious NPR has a comedy show that's a twenty-year-plus runaway national hit: *Wait Wait . . . Don't Tell Me!* with Peter Sagal.

Perhaps the depth and breadth of our recent cornucopia of comedy can be better appreciated by offering a few statistics. Since its beginnings in 1975, *Saturday Night Live* has had approximately 160 cast members and in excess of 580 guest hosts. Netflix has hosted in excess of 200 comedy specials and recently has started to produce a number of original sitcoms. HBO and Showtime have developed and shown well over 55 comedy specials. Since the 1990s, Comedy Central has developed and hosted over 115 specials and sitcoms. In the last five years, network TV has produced more than 50 sitcoms in trying to stay competitive with their cable rivals. And finally, let's not forget that the age of the Internet and the art of podcasting have also greatly contributed both quantitatively and qualitatively to our collective interest in and appetite for comedy. PodcastInsights.com estimates that there are over 750,000 various podcasts. *Fast Company* puts the figure closer to 525,000 active podcasts and well over 18.5 million episodes to choose from.

Comedy is the most popular type of podcast, and the king of comedy podcasting is Marc Maron. Starting in 2009 and now with over one thousand episodes to his credit, Maron went from being a working comic getting by to such a cause célèbre that a sitting president of the United States, Barack Obama, reached out and asked whether Maron would invite him onto the podcast and interview him. This funny boom has produced an endless smorgasbord of comedy across all media platforms. And Conan O'Brien has jokingly said that he believed that "thirty-three percent of the American economy is now [based on] comedy!"[1] Actually, he may not be that far off.

Trivia nerd, *Jeopardy!* quiz show champion, and comedy lover Ken Jennings agrees that we live in a rapid-fire, joke-saturated society and that comedy is now the dominant voice in our culture. He refers to this phenomenon as "Planet Funny" and argues that it goes a lot deeper than the increased joke count per minute in half-hour sitcoms (in the 1950s, 2.5 jokes per minute; today, 6.38 jokes per minute) and the explosion of comedy specials on cable TV.[2] For Jennings, our so-called golden age is really an "excessive age of comedy," and we are all in danger of "killing ourselves with laughter" in a media blitz of jokes, political satire, comedic sound bites, witty commercials, and endless mindless shtick!

Jennings's lament is not only that humor, comedy, joke telling has become a major part of show business, TV, and clubs but also that the comedic outlook has seeped into every corner of our own public and commercial life. Worse yet, says Jennings, we are now used to it, expect it, and whether we like it or not, there's no escaping it. Clever repartee, whimsical badinage, sarcastic commentary, smart double entendres, and glib cynical snipes are now standard parts of our dialogical landscape. From greeting cards to news commentaries to instructional manuals to political ads to every aspect of commercial marketing and advertisement—comedy is king. Comedy is everywhere. Nothing is written or said without a carefully crafted clever or charmingly humorous embellishment or flourish.

In his 1963 marketing classic *Confessions of an Advertising Man*, David Ogilvy wrote, "Good copywriters have always resisted the temptation to entertain."

For Ogilvy, the ad industry had one absolute categorical: "Humor or fun will distract from the brand! Even if a customer got the joke, it didn't mean they would buy the product!"[3] Long before Ogilvy recanted on his "no-humor" rule, the industry had abandoned it, and every advertiser who could afford the outrageous production fees were trying to hire the services of people like Stan Freberg, the "father of the funny commercial" and winner of twenty-one Clio Awards for innovation and creative excellence in advertising. Freberg proved that a joke, wry, comical word play, or a funny jingle wasn't a "distraction." Rather, the "joke" was the hook that captured the potential customer's interest. For Freberg, comedy was the conduit to commerce. Comedy primed the pump for creating product desire and sales. It even became the motto of his ad agency: "Ars Gratia Pecuniae"—"Art for Money's Sake!"[4] Communications scholar Neil Postman loosely referred to this phenomenon as "infotainment." The joke or comic bit was the "whimsical wink" that alerted the target audience to the brand or the product, which could potentially result in a sale. The joke wasn't being told for the sake of art; the joke was an attempt to arrest the attention of potential customers for the sake of money. On average, Americans see about 362 paid media ads a day, about 200 of which use humor to convey their message. In 2014, it was estimated that over 52 percent of all advertisement in America was funny or lighthearted in nature. And "funny advertisements" are now annually a $60 billion business. That's *billion* with a capital *B*![5]

The principle of "infotainment" is no laughing matter! Indeed, we actually think it is a rather ironic turn of events. While we could go with a dictionary definition of irony ("When the outcome of events is contrary to, or incongruous with, what was or might have been expected"), we prefer to cite a more definitive source: George Carlin, lexicologist extraordinaire! He wrote,

> *If a diabetic, on his way to buy insulin, is killed by a runaway truck, he is the victim of an accident. If the truck was delivering sugar, he is the victim of an oddly poetic coincidence. But if the truck was delivering insulin, ah ha! Then he is the victim of an irony.*[6]

To beat the point to death, please consider two other elegant examples of "cosmic irony": Adolph Coors III was allergic to beer! And fitness guru and long-distance runner Jim Fixx died of a heart attack while jogging![7] Similarly, there's nothing really funny about the serious business of making money!

Other classic examples of *ars gratia precuniae*/infotainment are easy to come across:

- Stan Freberg's classic 1960 Sunsweet Prunes jingle: "Today the pits, tomorrow the wrinkles!"

- The Budweiser Frogs, who were introduced to American audiences during the 1995 Super Bowl

- Reebok's "Terry Tate, Office Linebacker" campaign of 2003

And of course there is the insurance industry's mini-boom of comedic advertisements:

- Geico's Caveman ad, beginning in 2004 and later made into a short-lived sitcom, *Cavemen*, in 2007

- Geico's Camel and the "Hump Day!" commercial, from early 2012 to early 2013

- Geico's Gecko "Spokes-Lizard," first appearing in 2000

- The Aflac Duck, which hit the airwaves in December 1999

- Progressive's spokesperson Flo, beginning in late 2008

- Allstate's Mayhem Man, beginning in June 2010

According to Jennings, and as we have been arguing and detailing, there are two central sustaining causes of our contemporary social/political comedy tsunami. The first is Jon Stewart and his long lineage of acolytes, and the other eight-hundred-pound gorilla in the room is Donald

Trump and his victory in the 2016 Republican primary and subsequent surprising election as the forty-fifth president of the United States. (NB: "Political correctness" requires us to point out that the use of the term "gorilla" is intended as a simple literary phrase or figure of speech and not a reflection of our political point of view regarding Mr. Trump. Except, of course, it really is!)

Jon Stewart took over *The Daily Show* in 1999. As we have already discussed, the show is not a "real news" show. The intentional conceit of the program is that it is "faking," "pretending," and "comically playing" at being a news show. The news itself is "real," but the job of the show is not to report on it, but rather to make fun of it and ridicule it. Essentially, playing the combined role of a comic-political reporter and serious pundit, Stewart took on the nightly task of mocking and chastising almost everyone and everything in the news and society at large. No one—not Democrats, Republicans, liberals, conservatives, Libertarians, vegetarians, Tea Party members, teetotalers, polygamists, xenophobes, the various candidates in the Republican presidential primary race, the pope, or autoerotic-asphyxiation devotees—was above or beyond the reach of his commentary and criticism.

Stewart's tenure on the program proved to be both a professional and a popular success. In the course of sixteen years, Stewart garnered twenty-two Emmy Awards and was the voice of a new "news" generation. He was the closest thing that millennials and late Gen Xers had to the dual legends of truth telling and news reporting Walter Cronkite and Edward R. Murrow. And let's not forget, he's a comedian and not a reporter!

For Jennings, and as we have also argued, the other central and sustaining reason for the comedic saturation of all forms of our media outlets is the election of Donald J. Trump as the forty-fifth president of the United States. Putting aside partisan politics and personal political predilections, love him or hate him, we are fascinated by Trump's demeanor, his brashness and braggadocio, his idiosyncratic comments, his iconoclastic pronouncements, his writ-large unorthodox behavior, his over-the-top style and manner. Trump is a natural target for media scrutiny and a catalyst for controversy. And as presidential historian Daniel Boorstin has pointed out, "An image . . . becomes all the more interesting with our every effort to debunk it." The very qualities that appall Trump's comic detractors keep us (the audience) riveted to the spectacle of his presidency.[8] CNN has suggested that the "Age of Trump" has affectively altered the format and content of late-night TV and perhaps the very nature of political comedy and satire.[9]

Ken Jennings's thesis in *Planet Funny* is a straightforward one: "Comedy is the dominant voice of our culture."[10] If he's right, and we think he is, how does that affect our relationship with humor/comedy and its use in our lives? Let's begin by looking at two quotes from Mark Twain that have offered comfort and consolation to many students of comedy:

Against the assault of laughter, nothing can stand.[11]

Humor is the great thing, the saving thing.[12]

Jennings points out Twain's maxims no longer apply or offer comfort in a world awash with frivolity and saturated with clever phrases, political satire, and daily mega-doses of sitcom joke telling. And then, lest we forget, there's the joke lists you can find online and the barrage of jokes that come to us via social media. Plus, there's laughter yoga classes, laughter therapy groups, funny and constantly funnier TV commercials and magazine ads, clever appliance manuals, cheerful pharmaceutical commercials and instructions, silly birthday cards, funny get-well cards, perky condolence cards, whimsical billboards, and catchy radio jingles. Jennings asks, "What's next: ironic eulogies, funny headstones, jokes on traffic signs, jokes in scientific and medical journals, funny insurance policies, clever wills and hilarious death notices?"[13] Jennings argues that rather than being a stimulant, a catalyst, for greater awareness and a meaningful response to life, humor has become an "acceptable opiate," our "drug of choice" that allows us to overlook or more easily tolerate reality. Instead of being a corrective tool or a weapon against reality, humor has become a narcotic that wears us down, wears us out, and anesthetizes us.

Jennings warns that when playful humor becomes the dominant mode of discourse, we become disconnected from more important issues in life. He argues that even political humor that is specifically intended to be satirically subversive often winds up being counterproductive. Instead of potentially mobilizing individuals into action, jokes can become "convenient escape valves," a way for unhappy people to let off steam and feel better about their lot without actually fighting back against oppression. For example, late-night satirical monologues are on at bedtime. Most of us don't watch someone make fun of a "bad political player" and then feel immediately empowered and mobilized to call our local senator or congressman or volunteer for a nonprofit. No, we hear the joke, and if we are in agreement with the joke, we feel deep satisfaction and then immediately drop off to sleep! Bottom line: Too often, in a joke-/humor-saturated society, we learn to laugh at problems rather than solve them. We seek immunity from life through humor.[14]

We think Jennings is on to something and that the "accelerating crescendo" of humor in our culture is cause for real concern. His critique and admonitions should be listened to and addressed. Although we concur that humor alone is inadequate to make life meaningful, we are nevertheless convinced that the correct use of humor is a valid "survival strategy" that can at least offer us hope. Humor cannot provide ultimate answers or even adequate resolution of life's endless parade of difficulties, mysteries, and questions. Nor will the practice of humor ("being funny") necessarily make you a better person. But humor can offer temporary distraction, solace, and hope and perhaps, just perhaps, on occasion a transcendent moment of understanding. It can also puncture the self-seriousness of sanctimony that has its own political pathologies when left unchecked. To paraphrase the words of journalist Steve Lipman, although often heartbreakingly inadequate, humor and joke telling are a "currency of hope" in the midst of a confusing and chaotic world.[15]

The Renaissance scholar and philosopher Desiderius Erasmus of Rotterdam (1466–1536) published an essay titled "In Praise of Folly," arguing that all human relationships—government, business, the church, marriage, and friendship—require folly, the goddess of all things "silly and lighthearted." For Erasmus, without the foolishness and fun of folly, "no society, no union in life could be either pleasant or long-lasting." Humor makes life more agreeable, more attractive, and more sustainable. Like the moderate use of alcohol, humor can prove comforting and curative in regard to many of life's challenges. But in excess, humor (again like alcohol) can be addictive, debilitating, demeaning, and destructive.[16] Nobody likes the braggart, the nonstop verbal bully, or the blustering fool. The excessive use of humor can prove to be humor's own undoing and antithesis. Too many jokes, "too much folly," dilutes the pleasure and effectiveness of joke telling.

Although the Trump presidency has made political comedy/satire "great" again and has increased the viewership of late-night, comedic TV, the danger of comedic success is comedic excess and saturation. And worse still, comedy can make us callous to the real issues and problems around us. And instead of dealing with problems, we learn to laugh at them rather that attack them or solve them. We self-medicate with humor in order not to deal with a situation or problem. Too often, we use laughter, humor, and joke telling as a form of denial or escapism.[17] Clearly, we are in need of an alternative approach.

On the very last page of *Planet Funny*, Ken Jennings offers a "modest proposal" to keep in check our cultural propensity to use humor as our central coping device for dealing with reality:

Let's keep some part of the public sphere laughter-optional, so that serious engagement and earnest emotion don't become completely taboo. We can do this in small ways. We can advocate for things we believe sometimes, instead of satirically adopting the opposite

*view. We can supplement our diet of comedy news
shows with actual journalism. We can ensure that
our decisions—as both consumers and citizens—are
based on the merits of the products or issues or candidates involved, not just on the funny messaging. We
can take breaks from social media, so our brains don't
settle on hundreds of jokes an hour as the new normal.
We can spend time in nature, which hasn't gotten
notably funnier since the platypus evolved twenty million years ago.*

*We can look for chances to talk about things we
enjoy, not just ridicule the things we don't. We can ask
ourselves what others need to hear, not what we could
amuse ourselves by saying. We can genuinely listen to
them, rather than look for openings to crack jokes. We
can acknowledge compliments instead of deflecting
them with nervous quips. We can skip the affectionate
jabs and roasts sometimes and just tell the people we
love how much they mean to us.[18]*

Bottom line: It's not either/or. It's not "joking versus
not joking." It's not "satire verses sincerity." Rather, what
Jennings is arguing for is a balance of sincerity and satire. Otherwise a word play on the title of Neil Postman's
book may be the perfect epithet on our collective tomb-
stone: "We Amused Ourselves to Death." The late Nobel
Laureate Toni Morrison was convinced that our use of

language and laughter determines the quality of our lives lived with others. What we say and how we say it sets the tone and establishes the meter for the possibility of civility, consensus, and comedic relief with those we choose to live with and love.

NOTES

PROLOGUE

1. Terry Eagleton, *Humour* (New Haven, CT: Yale University Press, 2019), 41.

2. R. Chand Lord, "Margaret Cho, Stand-up Comic on Hong Kong Lessons, Trump Jokes, and the Virtues of Courting Danger in Singapore," *South China Morning Post*, May 1, 2018.

3. Steve Johnson, "Late Night TV Confronts a Tough Question: Are Democratic Candidates Funny?" *Chicago Tribune*, June 28, 2019, http://www.chicagotribune.com/entertainment/tv/ct -ent-late-night-colbert-democratic-debates-0701-20190628 -ewc56olv4fcibnehvop7nls3ky-story.html.

4. Robert Trachtenberg, dir., *Mel Brooks: Make a Noise*, American Masters Series (PBS, 2013).

CHAPTER 1

1. Dan Kois, "Unfrozen Cerebral Humorist," *New York Times Magazine*, July 21, 2013, 22, 24, 25.

2. David Marchese, "Talk: Ricky Gervais," *New York Times Magazine*, March 24, 2019, 23–25.

3. Ibid.

4. Gershon Legman, *Rationale of the Dirty Jokes: An Analysis of Dirty Humor* (New York: Simon & Schuster, 1996).

5. "Is Trump Good for Comedy? Comedians Respond," *Washington Post*, July 13, 2017, https://www.washingtonpost .com/news/arts-and-entertainment/wp/2017/07/13/is-trump-good -for-comedy-comedians-respond.

6. Lewis Black, *Rant, White, and Blue Tour* (New York: Live Nation/MSG Production, April 28, 2017).

7. Ibid.

8. "Election Ushered in Altered D.C. Reality," *Chicago Tribune*, Arts and Entertainment, April 12, 2017, 5.

9. Ibid.

10. Zeke Miller, "Trump Attacks Cummings' District," *Chicago Tribune*, Section 1, July 28, 2019, 21.

11. Ibid.

12. Ibid.

13. Ibid.

14. Chris Jones, "Who Is the Real Carnival Barker? Donald Trump or John Oliver?" *Chicago Tribune*, June 12, 2018, https://www.chicagotribune.com/entertainment/theater/ct-jones-trump-ae-0313-20160311-column.html.

15. Steve Johnson, "Late-Night TV Confronts a Tough Question: Are Democratic Candidates Funny?" *Chicago Tribune*, June 28, 2019, https://www.chicagotribune.com/entertainment/tv/ct-ent-late-night-colbert-democratic-debates-0701-20190628-ewc56olv4fcibnehvop7nls3ky-story.html.

16. Sarah Taylor, "Alec Baldwin Asked Donald Trump to Guest Star on SNL," May 4, 2017, https://www.theblaze.com/news/2017/05/04/alec-baldwin-asked-donald-trump-to-guest-star-on-snl-he-now-has-the-presidents-answer.

17. Clarence Page, "How Donald Trump Made Political Comedy Great Again," *Chicago Tribune*, Section 1, November 18, 2018, 27.

18. "5 Comedians Who Got in Trouble for 9/11 Comments," *Paste Magazine*, September 5, 2015, https://www.pastemagazine.com/articles/2015/09/5-comedians-who-got-in-trouble-for-911-comments.html.

19. "Goofy Movies Number Six," IMDB, http://imdb.com/title/tt0142328.

20. "Indecision 2000," *The Daily Show*, Comedy Central, August 3, 2000, http://www.cc.com/video-clips/p26yji/the-daily-show-with-jon-stewart-indecision-2000—-convention-highlights.

21. David Itzkoff, "John Oliver Returns: I'm Not a Complete Nihilist," *New York Times*, February 7, 2017, https://www.nytimes.com/2017/02/07/arts/television/john-oliver-returns-im-not-a-complete-nihilist.html.

22. Paul Farhi, "And Now, the (Fake) News," *Chicago Tribune*, Arts and Entertainment, Section 4, April 7, 2014, 3.

23. "Comics Mock Trump at Fundraiser for Vets," Associate Press Report, *Chicago Tribune*, Section 4, November 9, 2017, 2.

24. Terry Gross, "Comic Hasan Minhaj on Roasting Trump and Growing Up a 'Third Culture Kid,'" *Fresh Air*, NPR, May 18, 2017, https://www.npr.org/2017/05/18/528936208/comic-hasan-minhaj-on-roasting-trump-and-growing-up-a-third-culture-kid.

25. Susan Dominus, "Hasan Minhaj Thinks Comedy Is for Weirdos," *New York Times Magazine*, Talk Section, June 25, 2017, 66.

26. Pew Research Center, "What Studies Say about Satire," "The Intersection of Politics and Satire: A Moment Symposium," *Moment*, November 1, 2012, http://momentmag.com/how-does-satire-influence-politics.

27. Xiaoxia Cao, "Political Comedy Shows and Knowledge about Primary Campaigns: The Moderating Effects of Age and Education," *Mass Communication and Society* 11, no. 1 (2008): 43–61, http://dx.doi.org/10.1080/15205430701585028; Judy Baumgartner and Jonathan S. Morris, "The Daily Show Effect," *American Political Research* 34, no. 3 (2006), https://journals.sagepub.com/doi/10.1177/1532673X05280074.

28. Adam Gopnik, "Trying (and Failing) Not to Fear So Much about Trump," *New Yorker*, February 17, 2017, https://www.newyorker.com/news/daily-comment/trying-and-failing-not-to-fear-so-much-about-trump.

29. Mel Brooks, *The Screening of Young Frankenstein* (New York: Live Nation / MSG Production, May 27, 2017).

30. Walter Moss, "Mark Twain's Progressive and Prophetic Political Humor," *Hollywood Progressive*, July 27, 2012, http://hollywoodprogressive.com/mark-twain.

CHAPTER 2

1. Robert Trachtenberg, dir., *Mel Brooks: Make a Noise*, American Masters Series (PBS, 2013).

2. Philip Kerr, *Metropolis* (New York: G.P. Putnam's Sons, 2019), 364.

3. Ben Greenman, "Was It Something I Said?" review of *The Joker: A Memoir*, by Andrew Hudgins, *New York Times*, Sunday Book Review, July 5, 2013, https://www.nytimes.com/2013/07/07/books/review/the-joker-a-memoir-by-andrew-hudgins.html.

4. Al Gini, *The Importance of Being Funny* (Lanham, MD: Rowman & Littlefield, 2017), xiii.

5. Greenman, "Was It Something I Said?"

6. Eugen Fink, *Nietzsche's Philosophy*, trans. Goetz Richter (New York: Continuum, 2003), 157.

7. André Comte-Sponville, *A Small Treatise on the Great Virtues: The Users of Philosophy in Everyday Life*, trans. Catherine Temerson (New York: Metropolitan Books, 2001), 221.

8. Ted Cohen, *Jokes: Philosophical Thoughts on Joking Matters* (Chicago: University of Chicago Press, 1999), 44, 45.

9. Ricki Stern and Anne Sandberg, dirs., *Joan Rivers: A Piece of Work* (DVD, IFC Films, 2010).

10. Jerry Seinfeld, *Comedians in Cars Getting Coffee*, Guest: Bill Maher, June 24, 2015, Netflix.

11. Ibid.

12. Christopher Backley, "Booze as Muse," Sunday Review, Opinion, *New York Times*, June 29, 2013, http://nytimes.com/2013/06/30/opinion/sunday/booze-as-muse.html.

13. Paul Provenza and Dan Dion, *¡Satiristas! Comedians, Contrarians, Raconteurs and Vulgarians* (New York: It Books, 2010), 12, 13, 19, 20.

14. James Geary, *Wit's End* (New York: W. W. Norton, 2019), 2.

15. Paul Provenza and Dan Dion, *¡Satiristas!*, 279.

16. Jane Ogburn and Peter Backroyd, *Satire* (Cambridge: Cambridge University Press, 2013), 15.

17. Greenman, "Was It Something I Said?"

18. Terry Gross, interview with Bob Mankoff on his book *How about Never: Is Never Good for You?*, *Fresh Air*, NPR, April 14, 2017.

19. Ogborn and Buckroyd, *Satire*, 11–17.

20. Provenza and Dion, *¡Satiristas!*, 138.

21. Andrew Hudgings, *The Joker: A Memoir* (New York: Simon & Schuster, 2013), 102.

22. Orgborn and Buckroyd, *Satire*, 12.

23. Provenza and Dion, *¡Satiristas!*, 138.

24. Ibid., 96.

25. Mark Twain, "Facts and Summary," History.com, http://history.com/topics/mark-twain.

26. Paul Mersbarger, "Twain the Showman," unpublished paper/lecture, Loyola University Chicago, 1985.

27. Mark Twain, "Quotes by Mark Twain," All Poetry, 2010, http://allpoetry.com/quote/by/Mark%20Twain.

28. Greg Mitchell, "Will Rogers: Tribute to a Political Hero at the 75th Anniversary of His Death," *Huffington Post*, August 16, 2010, https://www.huffpost.com/entry/tragic-day-for-america -wh_b_683284.

29. P. J. Brian and Lovell Thomas, *Will Rogers: Ambassador of Good Will* (Whitefish, MT: Kessinger, 1935).

30. James Curtis, *Last Man Standing: Mort Sahl and the Birth of Modern Comedy* (Jackson: University of Mississippi Press, 2017), 137.

31. Tristin Hopper, "Mort Sahl Invented Stand-up Comedy— So What's He Doing at a Community Theatre in California?" *National Post*, https://nationalpost.com/entertainment/weekend -post/mort-sahl-invented-stand-up-comedy-so-whats-he-doing-at-a -community-theatre-in-northern-california.

32. Kliph Nesteroff, *The Comedians: Drunks, Thieves, Scoundrels, and the History of American Comedy* (New York: Grove Press, 2015), 161.

33. Hopper, "Mort Sahl Invented Stand-up Comedy."

34. Richard Zuglin, *Comedy at the Edge* (New York: Bloomsburg, 2008–2009), 9.

35. Curtis, *Last Man Standing*, 95, 136–37.

36. Lenny Bruce, *How to Talk Dirty and Influence People*, with a preface by Lewis Black (Philadelphia: Da Capo Press, 2016), 7–8.

37. John Cohen, ed., *The Essential Lenny Bruce* (New York: Bell Publishing Company, n.d.), 232.

38. Bruce used this line often enough that it became a bit of a mantra for him. His point was that what he was talking about really wasn't at all funny, but he was using humor to bring it to the public's attention. This mantra became the title of a one-man play, *I'm Not a Comedian . . . I'm Lenny Bruce*, written and played by Ronnie Marmo (2018).

39. Carlin's original routine reproduced in Justin R. Erenkrantz, "George Carlin's Seven Dirty Words," Justin R. Erenkrantz (website), last modified August 20, 2010, https://www.erenkrantz.com/Humor/SevenDirtyWords.shtml. See also Jacques Steinberg, "Refusing to Coast on 7 Infamous Words," *New York Times*, Television, November 4, 2005, https://www.nytimes.com/2005/11/04/arts/television/refusing-to-coast-on-7-infamous-words.html.

40. George Carlin, *3x Carlin: An Orgy of George* (New York: Hachette Books, 2014), 9–10.

41. Nesteroff, *The Comedians*, 157.

CHAPTER 3

1. Sumerian fart joke.

2. Aristotle, *The Politics*, translated by Carnes Lord (Chicago: University of Chicago Press, n.d.).

3. Quoted in Richard Vine, "Robin Williams's Best-Loved Gags," *The Guardian*, August 12, 2014, https://www.theguardian.com/film/2014/aug/12/robin-williams-best-loved-gags.

4. Andrew Dalton, "Chicago Comic Hannibal Buress, Who Called Cosby a Rapist in 2014 Standup Act, Now Credited after His Conviction," *Chicago Tribune*, April 27, 2018, https://www.chicagotribune.com/entertainment/ct-hannibal-buress-cosby-conviction-20180427-story.html.

5. Dave Chappelle, Stan Lathan, Kimber Rickabaugh, and Jeff U'ren, *Dave Chappelle: Killin' Them Softly* (DVD, UrbanWorks Entertainment, 2003).

6. Virginia Heffernan, "Chappelle the Shape-Shifter Sits Still Long Enough to Chat," *New York Times*, February 10, 2006, https://www.nytimes.com/2006/02/10/arts/television/chappelle-the-shape shifter-sits-still-long-enough-to-chat.html.

7. David Roediger, "Guineas, Niggers, and the Dramas of Racialized Culture," *American Literary History* 7, no. 4 (1995): 654–68.

8. Aljean Harmetz, "Man of a Thousand Voices, Speaking Literally," *New York Times*, November 24, 1988, https://www.nytimes.com/1988/11/24/arts/man-of-a-thousand-voices-speaking-literally.html.

9. Quoted in Kimberly A. Yates, "When 'Keeping It Real' Goes Right," in *The Comedy of Dave Chappelle, Critical Essays*, ed. K. A. Wismiewski (Jefferson, NC: McFarland, 2009).

10. David Henry and Joe Henry, *Richard Pryor and the World That Made Him* (New York: Algonguin, 2013), 162–63.

11. Ibid., 166.

12. Sammy Basu, "Dialogic Ethics and the Virtue of Humor," *Journal of Political Philosophy* 7, no. 4 (1999): 378–403. It should be noted that much of this section is informed by Simon Lambek's excellent discussion, which we cite more directly later on.

13. "Jeremy McLellan: 77 Cents," video posted to YouTube by Jeremy McLellan on September 5, 2016, https://youtu.be/3wO77nbygr0.

14. Michael Barber and Jeremy C. Pope, "Does Party Trump Ideology? Disentangling Party and Ideology in America," *American Political Science Review* 113, no. 1 (2019): 38–54, doi:10.1017/S0003055418000795.

15. Meredith Blake, "Stephen Colbert Pays Tribute to Supreme Court Justice Antonin Scalia," *Los Angeles Times*, February 16, 2016, https://www.latimes.com/entertainment/tv/showtracker/la-et-st-stephen-colbert-react-to-the-death-of-justice-antonin-scalia-20160216-story.html.

16. Simon Lambek, "Receiving Rhetoric: Language and Democratic Politics" (PhD diss., University of Toronto, 2020).

17. Simone Chambers, "Deliberative Democratic Theory," *Annual Review of Political Science* 6, no. 1 (2003): 307–26.

18. John Moffitt, dir., *Talking Funny* (HBO, April 20, 2011).

19. Shaun King, "The Entire Speech: What, to the Slave, Is the 4th of July?" *Medium*, July 5, 2018, https://medium.com/@ShaunKing/the-entire-speech-what-to-the-slave-is-the-4th-of-july-d011fe7909f4.

CHAPTER 4

1. Barbara Holm, "Here Is What's Scary about Being a Female Stand-up Comic," *Bitch Media*, April 30, 2013, www.bitchmedia.org/post/here-is-whats-scary-about-being-a-female-stand-up-comic.

2. Richard Zoglin, *Comedy at the Edge* (New York: Bloomsbury, 2009), 192.

3. Chris Nashawaty, "Comedy Legend Jerry Lewis Dies at 91," *Entertainment Weekly*, August 20, 2017, https://ew.com/tv/2017/08/20/jerry-lewis-dead-comedy-legend-dies-at-91.

4. Brent Lang, "Cannes: Jerry Lewis Skewered for Latest Bad-Taste Sexist Remarks," *The Wrap*, May 29, 2013, https://www.thewrap.com/cannes-jerrylewis-skewered-latest-bad-taste-sexist-remarks-93656.

5. Eliana Dockterman, "Inside Amy Schumer and Broad City: Guys Watch Feminist Comedy," *Time*, April 1, 2014, http://time.com/45771/how-amyschumer-got-guys-to-think-feminists-are-funny.

6. Melissa Rivers with Scott Currie, *Joan Rivers Confidential* (New York: Abrahms, 2017), 44, 45, 46.

7. Ibid., 61.

8. Kathi Maio, "Roseanne," in *Revolutionary Laughter: The World of Women Comics*, ed. Roz Warren (Freedom, CA: Crossing Press, 1995), 196.

9. Ricki Stern and Anne Sundberg, dirs., *Joan Rivers: A Piece of Work* (DVD, IFC Films, 2010).

10. Joan Rivers with Valerie Frankel, *Men Are Stupid . . . and They Like Big Boobs* (New York: Pocket Books, 2009).

11. Ibid., 9.

12. Judith Newman, "From Sarah Silverman, an Adorable Look, Followed by a Sucker Punch," *New York Times*, May 7, 2010, http://nytimes.com/2010/05/09/fashion/09sarah.html.

13. Ibid.

14. Sophie Heawood, "Sarah Silverman: There Are Jokes I Made 15 Years Ago I Would Absolutely Not Make Today," *The Guardian*, November 19, 2017, https://www.theguardian.com/global/2017/nov/19/sarah-silverman-interview-jokes-i-made-15-years-ago-i-wouldnt-make-today.

15. Newman, "From Sarah Silverman."

16. Terry Gross, "Sarah Silverman: Turning Ignorance into Comedy," *Fresh Air*, NPR, April 22, 2010.

17. Sam Anderson, "Sarah Silverman Rapes American Comedy," *Slate Magazine*, November 10, 2005, http://slate.com/culture/2005/11/sarah-silverman-rapes-american-comedy.html.

18. Ibid.

19. Margaret Cho, *I Have Chosen to Stay and Fight* (New York: Riverhead Books, 2005), 20.

20. Ibid., 21, 22.

21. Margaret Cho, *I'm the One That I Want* (New York: Ballantine, 2001), 85.

22. Paul Provenza and Dan Diox, *¡Satiristas! Comedians, Contrarians, Raconteurs and Vulgarians* (New York: It Books, 2010), 326–28.

23. Cho, *I Have Chosen to Stay and Fight*, 77.

24. Ibid., 3.

25. Ibid., 181–82.

26. Ibid., 3.

27. Lee Siegal, *Groucho Marx* (New Haven, CT: Yale Press, 2015), 76.

28. Margaret Cho, stand-up routine at Improv Comedy Club, Orlando, Florida, JenCray, ink19.com, June 21, 2015.

29. Amy Schumer, *The Girl with the Lower Back Tattoo* (New York: Gallery Books, 2016), 26.

Chapter 5

1. Robert Menchin, *101 Classic Jewish Jokes* (Memphis, TN: Mustang Publishing, 1997), 12.

2. Jeremy Dauber, *Jewish Comedy: A Serious History* (New York: W. W. Norton, 2017), 10.

3. John Morreal, *Comedy, Tragedy, and Religion* (Albany: State University of New York Press, 1999), 94–99.

4. Sal Hoffman with Eric Spiegelman, *Old Jews Telling Jokes* (New York: Villard, 2010).

5. Philip Roth, *Goodbye Columbus* (Boston: Houghton Mifflin Harcourt, 1959), 41.

6. Michael Krasny, *Let There Be Laughter* (New York: William Morrow, n.d.), 47.

7. Dave Chappelle, *Age of Spin* (Los Angeles: Netflix, released March 21, 2017).

8. Devorah Baum, *The Jewish Joke* (New York: Pegasus Books, 2018), 30.

9. Ibid., 37.

10. Friedrich Nietzsche, *The Will to Power*, trans. A. M. Ludovici (Mineola, NY: Dover, 2019).

11. Robert Trachtenberg, dir., *Mel Brooks: Make a Noise*, American Masters Series (PBS, 2013).

12. Ibid.

13. Amy Sherman-Palladino, dir., "Mid-way to Mid-town," Season 2, Episode 2 of *The Marvelous Mrs. Maisel* (Amazon Video, Original Westwork, December 5, 2018).

14. Ferne Pearstein, dir., *The Last Laugh* (Pilgim, LLC [Netflix], 2016).

15. Ibid.

16. Paul E. McGhee, *Health, Healing, and the Amuse System: Humor as Survival Training*, 3rd ed. (Dubuque, IA: Kendall/Hunt, 1999), 20.

17. Paul E. McGhee, "Using Humor to Cope: Humor in Concentration/POW Camps," *The Laughter Remedy*, https://www

.laughterremedy.com/article_pdfs/Using%20Humor%20to%20Cope
-Part%202.pdf.

18. Rudolph Herzog, *Dead Funny: Telling Jokes in Hitler's Germany*, trans. Jefferson Chase (New York: Melville House, 2012), 6.

19. Pearstein, *The Last Laugh*.

20. Mevlut Akkaya and Ron Frank, dir., *When Comedy Went to School* (Catskills Films, LLC, 2013).

21. Al Gini, John Powers, and Aaron Freeman, "One Flight Up," *Humor and Stand-Up Comedy*, WBEZ, 91.5FM, Chicago Public Radio, May 6, 1992.

CHAPTER 6

1. David Galef, "What's Not Funny," *Common Review* 2, no. 1 (Winter 2002): 22–26.

2. Mark C. Weeks, "Laughter, Desire, and Time," *Humor* 15, no. 4 (November 2002): 383–400.

3. David Brenner, *I Think There's a Terrorist in My Soup: How to Survive Personal and World Problems with Laughter—Seriously* (Kansas City, MO: Andrews McMeel, 2003), 27.

4. Ted Cohen, *Jokes: Philosophical Thoughts on Joking Matters* (Chicago: University of Chicago Press, 1999), 12, 26–27.

5. Duncan McFarlane, "The Universal Literary Solvent: Northrop Frye and the Problem of Satire, 1942 to 1957," *ESC: English Studies in Canada* 37, no. 2 (2011): 153–72.

6. Cohen, *Jokes*, 61.

7. Scott Weems, *Ha! The Science of When We Laugh and Why* (New York: Basic Books, 2014), 23.

8. Ken Jennings, *Planet Funny* (New York: Scribner, 2018), 247.

9. Zach Freeman, "Louis C.K. Is Master of His Domain at Chicago Theatre," *Chicago Tribune*, Arts and Entertainment, June 2, 2016, http://www.chicagotribune.com/entertainment/theater/ct -louis-ck-chicago-theatre-ent-0603-20160602-story.html.

10. Jennings, *Planet Funny*, 246.

11. Steven Gimbel, *Isn't That Clever* (New York: Routledge, 2018), 166.

12. "C.K. Mocks Parkland Survivors Onstage," *Chicago Tribune*, Section 1, January 1, 2019, 10.

13. Scott Simon, "Opinion: Louis C.K. Can Say What He Wants, but At Least Be Funny," *Weekend Edition*, NPR, January 5, 2019, https://www.npr.org/2019/01/05/682361470/opinion-louis-c-k-can-say-what-he-wants-but-at-least-be-funny.

14. Arthur Koestler, *The Act of Creation* (New York: Arkana, 1989), 53.

15. Kimberle Crenshaw, "Mapping the Margins: Intersectionality, Identity Politics, and Violence against Women of Color," *Stanford Law Review* 43 (1990): 1241.

16. Garry Trudeau, "The Abuse of Satire," *The Atlantic* (April 2015), https://www.theatlantic.com/international/archive/2015/04/the-abuse-of-satire/390312.

17. David Remnick, "A Conversation with Al Franken on Trump, the Senate, and His DeHumorizer Machine," *New Yorker*, August 4, 2017, https://www.newyorker.com/news/news-desk/a-conversation-with-al-franken-on-trump-the-senate-and-his-dehumorizer-machine.

18. Jeremy McLellan, "Bombing Onstage: Comedy on Political Resistance," *Cato Unbound*, April 1, 2017, https://www.cato-unbound.org/2017/04/01/jeremy-mclellan/bombing-stage-comedy-political-resistance.

19. "Dave Chappelle | Kramer | Stand-Up Comedy," video posted to YouTube by Laugh Factory on December 20, 2010, https://www.youtube.com/watch?v=Kth0UOU5a_M.

CHAPTER 7

1. Ken Jennings, *Planet Funny: How Comedy Took Over Our Culture* (New York: Scribner, 2018), 109.

2. Ibid., 77–79, 86.

3. Ibid., 91.

4. Ibid., 92.

5. Ibid., 97–99, 111.

6. Ibid., 169.

7. Ibid., 168.

8. Jennifer Egan, "Facts Still Exist," *Time*, December 24–31, 2018, 128.

9. Chris Cuomo, *Cuomo Prime Time*, CNN, November 20, 2017.

10. Jennings, *Planet Funny*, 281.

11. Mark Twain, *The Mysterious Stranger and Other Stories* (Mineola, NY: Dover, 1992), 117.

12. Mark Twain, "What Paul Bouget Thinks of Us," in *The Writings of Mark Twain* (New York: Harper & Brothers, 1899), 22:163.

13. Jennings, *Planet Funny*, 257, 267.

14. Ibid., 268.

15. Ibid., 265.

16. Desiderius Erasmus, *In Praise of Folly*, trans. Hoy Hopewell Hudson (Princeton, NJ: Princeton University Press, 2015).

17. Jennings, *Planet Funny*, 272.

18. Ibid., 274, 275.

INDEX

stand-up comedy clubs, 156.
*See also specific stand-up
comedians*
Stewart, Jon: criticism of,
21–22; *The Daily Show*,
18–21, 22, 163; influence
of, 16, 162–64; on role of
humor, 31
Stiller, Jerry, 118
survival, 117–19
Swift, Jonathan, 38–39

taboo subjects, 127–28,
130–32
television comedies and
specials, 157–58. *See also
specific television shows*
timing of jokes, 124–25
The Tonight Show, 74, 75,
81
Trachtenburg, Robert, xiv
Trudeau, Gary, 139, 140,
148–49
Trump, Donald J.: comedy of,
69; effect on comedy, xi,
5–8, 12, 15–16, 162–63,
164; *SNL* portrayal of,

13; Stewart on, 8, 22–23;
tweets of, 10–11
Twain, Mark, 40, 41–42, 61,
63, 165

VEEP, 8–10, 12

Wait Wait . . . Don't Tell Me,
26, 157
Walls, Nancy, 21
West, Linda, 130–31
When Comedy Went to School,
118
Wilde, Oscar, 98
Williams, Robin, 56
Wilmore, Larry, 23–24
Wilson, Flip, 73
Wolcott, Greg, 155
Wolf, Michelle, 23–24, 68
women in comedy. *See* gender
and comedy; *specific female
comedians*

Youngman, Henny, 45, 71,
77, 110

zoon politikon, x, 54

About the Authors

Al Gini is professor of business ethics in the Quinlan School of Business at Loyola University Chicago. He is a cofounder and longtime associate editor of *Business Ethics Quarterly*, the journal of the Society for Business Ethics. For over twenty-seven years he was the resident philosopher for National Public Radio's Chicago affiliate, WBEZ-FM, and he can currently be heard on WGN/Tribune Radio. His most recent book is *The Importance of Being Funny: Why We Need More Jokes in Our Lives* (2018).

Abraham Singer is assistant professor of management at Loyola University Chicago. He holds a PhD in political science from the University of Toronto. His first book, *The Form of the Firm*, was published in 2019, and his articles have been published in journals like *Business Ethics Quarterly*, *Journal of Politics*, *Political Research Quarterly*, *Economics & Philosophy*, and *Journal of Business Ethics*.